GET PUBLISHED
WITHOUT GETTING RIPPED OFF

Ted Bowman

JC Publishers LLC
Winter Haven, Florida

Scripture quotations marked NASB are from the New American Standard Bible. Copyright© 1960, 1962, 1963, 1968, 1971, 1972, 1973, 1975, 1977 by the Lockman Foundation. Used by permission.

ISBN 13: 978-0-9796899-4-9
ISBN 10: 0-9796899-4-5

Printed and Bound in Canada

This is a JC Publishers trade paperback.

DEDICATION

This book is dedicated to the thousands of unsuspecting authors who have already been royally ripped off by a vanity publisher because they did not understand the business end of publishing. Consider it a lesson learned and keep writing. You can professionally publish your next book and bypass vanity publishers altogether by simply buying and using your own ISBN. Owning the ISBN also eliminates the need to sign a contract to get your book in print.

To those who dream of a book deal, I offer a how-to guide to help you attract a professional literary agent who will sell your manuscript to a traditional publisher. And maybe, just maybe, you will find that pot of gold at the end of the literary rainbow.

Contents

INTRODUCTION

You won't find anything new in this book. Publishing is publishing. What you will discover is a practical, how-to guide to expertly self-publish a book that meets modern publishing industry standards—*without overpaying and without signing a contract.* In short, this book will teach you the business end of publishing so your writing won't be in vain and your wallet won't be flat.

You can be a self-published author who owns all the rights to your book, and I mean *all* of them. You deserve to make 100% of the profit on each sale without sharing a penny with a greedy publisher that has no investment in your work.

For those of you who believe you are pregnant with the next bestseller, this book will teach you, step-by-step, how to secure a literary agent who will help you land a contract with a traditional publisher.

CHAPTER 1

FIRST THINGS FIRST

I hear it every time I speak at a local writers' group meeting. *I've finished my manuscript—now what?* I always ask, *Have you visited your local bookstore yet?* The response is the same every time: picture a bunch of motionless deers in headlights.

Here is what I tell every writer: *before you type another word, drop everything, go to your local bookstore and check out the competition.* Are you reinventing the wheel? Is your book unique or is it a cookie-cutter version of several other books on the same subject nobody is buying? Trust me, there are books out there similar to yours. A few are selling well—the rest, not so much.

Michael Hyatt, former CEO for Thomas Nelson Publishers, gets to the crux of the matter when he says, "Differentiating your book from others is critically important."[1]

THREE CRUCIAL QUESTIONS

Before you tap another computer key, put on your sneakers and visit two or three bookstores. While there, write down answers to three crucial questions:

(1) How many books did you find in your genre, your subject?

(2) Is your book just like the others?

(3) If your book is similar, what can you do to make it unique or better, so people will want to buy yours and leave the others on the shelf?

If you found several similar books already in print, you may want to rethink your project. Instead of, "How to make a wheel," perhaps you should rework your book to explain, "How to make a wheel that sings and dances." You get the picture. Don't get discouraged; think hard and come up with new ideas for what may be an old concept. "How do I come up with new ideas for a well-worn subject, Ted?"

I won't encourage you to plagiarize, but everybody does to some extent. *Plagiarize,* according to Webster, means: *to steal and pass off (the ideas or words of another) as one's own.*

Here is the question: *can you think of one original idea or theme that someone else hasn't already touched on?* Probably not. Can you write about a common subject and make it more interesting, more challenging, more gripping or more thought-provoking? Of course you can. There will always be an angle no one else has thought of or a fresh new way to express an old thought, idea, or concept.

In 1903 Mark Twain expressed his thoughts on plagiarism in a letter to his friend, Helen Keller, who had been accused of plagiarizing in one of her short stories. He wrote:

> *Oh, dear me, how unspeakably funny and owlishly idiotic and grotesque was that 'plagiarism' farce! As if there was much of anything in any human utterance, oral or written,*

2

except plagiarism! The kernel, the soul—let us go further and say the substance, the bulk, the actual and valuable material of all human utterances—is plagiarism. For substantially all ideas are second-hand, consciously and unconsciously drawn from a million outside sources . . .

He concluded his letter with: *These object lessons should teach us that ninety-nine parts of all things that proceed from the intellect are plagiarisms, pure and simple, and the lesson ought to make us modest. But nothing can do that.*[2]

THERE IS NOTHING NEW UNDER THE SUN

Most of what I understand about life, I gleaned from friends, family members, books, songs, comedians, motivational speakers, and a few of my favorite teachers and preachers. If you use someone else's unique idea, give them credit, then add to it in ways that flavor it with your voice and style. The wise man Solomon said, "There is nothing new under the sun" (Eccl. 1:9 NASB). He was right, but that doesn't mean you can't portray sunlight in a whole new way with a pen instead of a brush.

If you have already written a book, don't be afraid to reuse some of your own ideas.

If you quote someone word-for-word, get permission and use it to make your point. That adds credibility to your argument. Don't overdo it, though, or you will produce just another potentially boring reference work with too many quotes.

You have more fresh ideas than you realize. If you use someone else's thought or idea, get permission to use it, then give them credit and write your own take or opinion

3

on the subject.

If you are a Christian writer, you can quote from the King James Bible or other ancient writings to your heart's content. Who are you going to ask for permission? I don't think Solomon, King David, the Apostle Paul, or Socrates will mind. Quoting from most newer versions of the Bible requires written permission. One exception is the New American Standard Bible, which allows you to quote up to five hundred verses without asking. Research these areas thoroughly. When using someone else's words, it is not easier to get forgiveness than permission. It is unethical and sometimes illegal.

If you want to use a line from a song, you need permission from the rights-holder (usually a record label), and it will probably cost you. If you can't get permission, don't take the chance. You could get sued. Songs written a century ago are safe to quote because the author is probably seventy years deceased (unless the songwriter discovered the fountain of youth and is still singing).

IT WILL MOTIVATE YOU AS AN AUTHOR LIKE NOTHING ELSE

I offer one more suggestion before you go back to writing your masterpiece. I encourage every would-be author to think hard about creating a book proposal. It will motivate you as a writer like nothing else.

A good place to find a downloadable book proposal guide is http://michaelhyatt.com/writing-a-winning-book-proposal. Michael Hyatt offers his very popular downloadable template for fiction or non-fiction book proposals for only 19.97 USD each (both for $29.94).

As I mentioned, he is the former CEO for Thomas Nelson Publishers. They commercially publish about five hundred books each year and he knows what agents and publishers want to see in a proposal.

Another good source is a book by Terry Whalin: *BOOK PROPOSALS THAT SELL.* See it at http://www. terrywhalin.com. Terry is a seasoned author with over sixty published books. He was a former literary agent and is now acquisitions editor for Morgan James Publishing.

Why all this fuss about a book proposal? Even if you plan to self-publish and won't need a book proposal, writing one will tell you whether yours is a book worth writing. A well-constructed book proposal will give you a sense of purpose as a writer. It is a lot of work, but it will make writing your manuscript much easier. The proposal for my last book was thirty-two pages (and I self-published).

Patricia Fry, president of Spawn.org, says writing a book proposal should precede writing a book, and not writing a proposal is the first of ten publishing mistakes new authors make. Read her article at http://www. matilijapress.com/articles/10-publishing-mistakes.htm.

Writing a proposal can be a valuable teaching tool. It will force you to develop chapter titles and a one or two paragraph synopsis of each chapter. You will identify your potential target audience and explain in detail how your book will benefit them.

One word of caution: never say, *It's for everybody.* If you can't pinpoint your target audience, your book may be too general (boring).

YOU WILL NEED A MARKETING PLAN

A proposal also helps you develop your marketing plan. Whether you self-publish or land a traditional publishing contract, you will need a marketing plan in place long before your book goes to press.

Your proposal will also identify affinity groups that might be interested in your book: television and radio programs, magazines, professional and non-profit organizations, and any other media outlets that might interview you about your book or have you as a guest speaker.

I have another friend who has been interviewed numerous times on local television and radio programs dealing with child abuse (the subject of her book).

A book proposal will also require you to identify at least three other current books in your genre, along with the title, author, publisher, and publish date of each. Then you will detail comparisons and contrasts between each book and yours and show why yours is different (and better). You will conclude your proposal with two or three sample chapters.

A BOOK PROPOSAL WILL PUT A FIRE IN YOUR BELLY

If you take the initiative and make the effort, a book proposal will put a fire in your belly and give you a glimpse into your future as an author. It changed my whole attitude toward writing and I wouldn't trade the experience. Remember, successful people are those who are willing to do the things unsuccessful people won't do.

If you say, *I can,* you're right—you will. If you say, *I can't,* you're right again—you probably won't.

CHAPTER 2

DECISION TIME

I hear you saying, *All right, Ted. I've written a book proposal and you were right. I am more excited than ever about my book.* Or, you may be admitting, *Sorry, Ted, I didn't write a proposal and I hope you aren't mad at me.*

Relax, I'm not upset. It's your deal, not mine. You can still write and publish a good book. Remember, my goal is helping you get published without getting ripped off.

Either way, if your manuscript is complete, it brings us to the question: *now what?* In the following chapters, I'll be talking about editing, cover design, interior layout (old-pros call it *typesetting*), ISBNs (the long number on the barcode), and the difference between vanity publishing, true self-publishing, and traditional publishing. It is decision time (don't just flip a coin). *Should I self-publish, or should I pursue a contract with one of the big boys?*

To answer that question, one should understand the pros and cons of both options. As you decide which way to go, remember Yogi Berra's advice: "When you come to a fork in the road, take it."

We will compare self-publishing to traditional publishing so you can choose wisely. Actually, you can do both, but only one fork at a time. A book contract is possible even after you self-publish. A growing trend has traditional publishers keeping an eye out for self-published books that are selling well. The number of books published by traditional publishers is decreasing each year, while self-published books are on the rise, now outnumbering traditionally published books annually.

As a self-published author, you will pay for everything to publish your book and are totally responsible for all marketing and sales. If a traditional publisher offers you a contract, it will include an advance, and that publisher will bear all the cost of publishing your book (but you will still be responsible for most of the marketing).

If you self-publish, you pay; if you publish under contract with a traditional publisher, they pay. Unfortunately, the days are gone when new authors got six-figure advances and the publisher paid for all marketing and publicity.

SHE WAS AN INSTANT MILLIONAIRE

Today, non-fiction authors need a public platform to attract commercial (traditional) publishers. That means they are well-known, with good media exposure and public name and face recognition. Because of who they are, thousands of admirers will buy their book. Sarah Palin, for instance, sold one million copies of her non-fiction book, *Going Rogue*, before it even went to press. She was an instant millionaire. Not so fast; it won't be that easy for you. Sarah, I know, but who are you?

Let's take a look at how you, as an unknown author, would make money with a traditionally published non-fiction book.

Suppose your publisher decides your book should retail for twenty dollars. You would receive a royalty of one to two dollars per book, depending on your contract. Ten percent royalties are typical.

WAIT, THERE'S MORE

Bookstores get a minimum fifty percent discount. Now your $20 book is a $10 book (wholesale price) as far as the publisher is concerned, and your royalty becomes $1 per book. Wait, there's more. Your agent gets another 15%. What's left? A whopping $.85 per book.

Not bad if you sell a million copies (that's $850,000). Not so good if you only sell 8,000 ($6,800 in royalties), which is more typical for unknown authors. Oops, you can't quit your day job yet. While you are at it, go ahead and cancel that order for a special edition, wire-wheel Lexus, and tell the swimming pool people you will have to get back to them.

To be fair, there are those first-time novelists who sold lots of books and made lots of money. John Grisham has done quite well, but his first book, *A Time To Kill*, was rejected by 28 publishers before a small publisher took a chance and printed 5,000 copies.

Over time, it has sold over two million.

Right after *A Time To Kill* was published, he started writing his second novel, *The Firm*, which sold seven million copies, staying on the *New York Times* bestseller list just under a year. Several of his books later became hit movies, including *A Time To Kill* and *The Firm*. The rest is history. He probably quit his day job.

My mistake. He kept his day job. It's called writing for fun and profit. Mr. Grisham proved it never hurts to dream.

SERIOUSLY LOOK AT SELF-PUBLISHING

Unless you are convinced you are the next John Grisham, you should seriously look at self-publishing your book. Contrary to misinformation on the subject, it is very possible to attract a traditional publisher after you self-publish.

A close friend wrote a book on dreams several years ago. She sold a few thousand copies through her public speaking appearances at churches and conferences. A traditional publisher got wind of it and called her personally to offer her a contract. She signed on and is now a published author for a prominent Christian publisher. She received some nice royalty checks in the process.

True to the typical new author scenario, the publisher printed a few thousand books and six months later took the book out of print, but it is still available online as a print-on-demand book and e-book. She can still order copies for personal sales and has done well. The book is still selling, due to her personal marketing and sales effort.

HOW TO SELF-PUBLISH

I have a menu on my website titled "How To Self-publish." It will help you understand a rather simple process that has been complicated by unscrupulous publishers looking to take advantage of unsuspecting authors. We will discuss these steps one by one. As I heard Rik Feeney say, *This is not rocket surgery.* Here's how it works:

1. Buy your own ISBN (this is huge).
2. Hire a professional book editor.
3. Hire a professional cover designer.
4. Hire an interior layout expert.
5. Get it printed at a reasonable cost.
6. Make it available to online bookstores.
7. Get it delivered and start selling.

It is a little more involved than that, but not much. There are publishers who will help you through the process, *a la carte,* and they are the true self-publishing companies (I like to call them self-publishing *facilitators*). You just order and pay for each service without signing a contract.

Look at it this way: do you sign a contract when you buy a book online? No, you just order and pay for the book. The same is true when you order publishing services from the right publisher.

The trick is finding a publisher that will accommodate you with reasonable pricing and quality service. Certain publishers will treat you fairly without taking advantage of your inexperience as an author. They are in the minority. The resource pages in the back of this book list several publishers I have personally communicated with and found them to be candid and honest. I self-published with two of them.

THEY GOT SNOOKERED

Many authors think they have self-published and are totally unaware that they are not self-published authors because they do not own the ISBN. More about that in the next chapter on ISBNs. They got snookered by a vanity publisher, lately referred to as an *Indie publisher*. The vanity leopard is trying to change its spots, but your bank account is still the prey.

A vanity publisher is a publisher who produces a book wholly at the author's expense. In other words, you pay for the whole enchilada. The idea is this: I pay to have my book published so I can enjoy the *vanity* of seeing my name listed on the cover as the author.

How can I identify a vanity publisher so I don't get ripped off?

That is a simple question with an even simpler answer. Tell any self-publisher you talk to that you plan on using your own ISBN. Those who object and say they can't allow that are vanity publishers. And don't believe the bogus reasons they give to persuade you to let them "assign" an ISBN. None of the given reasons will benefit you. Those few publishers who say, *Yes, you can use your own ISBN,* are true self-publishing facilitators and will usually treat you right. These companies help you become the actual publisher of your book by using *your* ISBN.

I took the safe route. I self-published my first book with my own ISBN. If it sells over time and a traditional publisher hears about it and offers me a contract, I will seriously consider it. Since I am aware of the scant numbers for new authors, I will not be chomping at the bit to sign if the opportunity comes my way. If my book is doing well, who's to say I can't just keep on selling and continue to make all the profit?

I have some friends who wrote a little book about upper cervical chiropractic care, and they are living comfortably off the royalties. They self-published and share the profit with no one. They even prepared the print-ready files that go directly to the printer and reprint for less than fifty cents per book. That same book, printed by a vanity publisher, would cost around three dollars each (the difference going into the vanity publisher's pocket).

THE SIMPLE DIFFERENCE BETWEEN TRADITIONAL AND VANITY PUBLISHERS

Here is the simple difference between traditional and vanity publishers. Traditional publishers want to sell lots of books to the reading public. Otherwise, they don't make any money.

Vanity publishers want to sell lots of books to the author. Otherwise, they don't make any money. If the book sells, they make even more money on the printing. They know the average self-published book doesn't sell that many copies and they don't care. They target the author for extra services and make a good profit off the "publishing package" the author purchases and the first hundred books the author buys for resale. With the inflated retail price, vanity publishers make an extra $400 to $600 on the first print run.

Rik Feeney, who recently spoke at our local writers'

group meeting, has published a number books, ten of them with traditional publishers and one with a major publisher. He now self-publishes most of his books, because he has a good public platform and can generate sales through his personal appearances and his website.

In our meeting he told us, "Five percent of the effort is writing and publishing; ninety-five percent is marketing and promotion."

PUBLISHERS SAVE THEIR BIG MARKETING BUCKS

Whether you self-publish or get picked up by a traditional publisher, you are still responsible for most (if not all) of the marketing and promotion. Yes, a traditional publisher will get your book on bookshelves everywhere and people will buy it. Beyond that, traditional publishers spend little money on marketing. They save their big marketing bucks for the John Grishams of the publishing world.

Question: would you rather make $.85 per book on 8,000 books while a traditional publisher makes the bulk of the profit? Or, would you rather make $5 per book on 3,000 books you self-published and sold all by yourself? And you didn't have to pay an agent. Do the math. You might want to call the swimming pool people back and tell them you are ready to dive in.

About getting your book on bookshelves: only 25% of your total sales will come from books purchased in brick-and-mortar bookstores. The other 75% will come from online sales, your personal appearances, and other sources like your website and blogs.

In other words, the books you sell personally will

provide the bulk of your writing income.

Next we will talk about the role of the ISBN and why personal ISBN ownership is essential when you self-publish.

CHAPTER 3

THE MONEY FUNNELS THROUGH THE ISBN

"If you don't own the ISBN," as Ron Pramschufer says, "you don't own squat." *ISBN*, by the way, stands for International Standard Book Number, the 13-digit number in both the Ingram and Bowker Books in Print databases that bookstores use to order books. It identifies the industry (books) the language, the publisher and the book title. Who owns that number is crucial because the money funnels through the ISBN. If you own it, all the profit funnels to you; if the publisher owns it, half the profit (your money) goes to the publisher. Wake up and smell the barcode.

IT MAKES MY BLOOD BOIL

Writing this chapter made my blood pressure spike because it makes my blood boil when I hear the ridiculous arguments vanity/Indie publishers use to convince authors they shouldn't use their own ISBN. You see, most of the money these book mills make on new authors is from the publishing rights and additional, often unnecessary services they try to sell you for marketing like posters, press releases, post cards, bookmarks, and on and

17

on and on as your money meter peaks into the red.

These add-ons are costly, will have little effect on actual sales, and your book still won't magically appear on bookshelves. Or, you could go online and buy John Kremer's *1001 Ways to Market Your Book*, and do all the marketing yourself. Kremer's book will set you back $27.95 with free shipping. It will teach you how to do practical things to successfully market your book (the same things vanity publishers charge thousands for).

ALL THE MONEY FUNNELS TO YOU

Here is the single most important fact about the ISBN: whoever owns the ISBN owns the publishing rights. To be a true self-publisher, you must own the ISBN. You will then be the publisher of record. All the money funnels to you, none of it going to some vanity publisher who has zero investment in your book.

If some publisher owns the ISBN, you will pay that publisher twice. You will personally fund everything up front to get your book in print. Then you will pay three or four dollars more than necessary for each book you print because they own the ISBN and you don't. I will explain why that is a dumb deal by asking two questions.

Would you buy a car, drive it a few years until it has some equity, and then sell it for a profit? Smart people do just that. Instead of putting that money in your pocket, would you track down the salesman who sold you the car and split the profit with him? Not if you have at least two brain cells to rub together.

If you don't own the ISBN, that is exactly what you

will do for the publisher who, as I've already said, has no investment in your book. You wind up giving the publisher a piece of the action on every book. That is why that publisher wants to "assign a unique ISBN." It is a rip-off. I can hear you saying, *But, Ted, they were so nice!*

I'll be even nicer if you pay me up front for a new Cadillac and don't mind when I deliver a dune buggy.

THAT DIRTY LITTLE SECRET

The ISBN does identify your book. It also identifies the vanity publisher. It's your book, but the publisher owns the publishing rights. (So much for the claim, "You own all the rights to your book.") Every order for the book goes through that publisher and so does a chunk of your money. They would rather you didn't know that dirty little secret.

They make their money off inexperienced, uninformed authors, because they know the average self-published book sells two hundred or fewer copies. That is the hard truth. They have one shot at helping you max out your credit cards and they are armed with smooth talk and unbelievable discounts you just can't afford to pass up. And there is always a special offer that has a time limit and a warning: "Tomorrow will be too late."

Don't bite. That salesperson will tell another author the same thing the day after tomorrow.

If you email or phone any vanity/indie publisher, let them know you will be using your own ISBN. You may have to tell them ten times, but eventually they will get the message and leave you alone.

ONE VANITY PUBLISHER BELITTLED ME

I'm amused at the bogus reasons they give to make you believe you are better off letting them assign an ISBN. The reasons include minimizing the importance of who owns the ISBN (if it's unimportant who owns it, then why can't I?) to emphasizing how difficult it is for an author to buy a single ISBN. It's not difficult at all.

One vanity publisher belittled me for not wanting to be identified with them as a "recognized publisher."

Are you kidding me? The one thing you don't want is a vanity publisher's name and logo on your book. Bookstores won't stock it because they don't trust the editing or the overall quality, and bookstore managers know who those vanity publishers are.

There is never a good reason to let them assign an ISBN to you. They lead you to believe it is your ISBN—it isn't. It belongs to them and so will you if you fall for their slick sales pitch.

THERE IS NO SUCH THING AS AN ASSIGNED ISBN

Always remember, there is no such thing as an assigned ISBN. It either belongs to you or it doesn't. You may be wondering, *Ted, why are you going on about the ISBN?* It saddens me, the number of authors I have admonished to get their own ISBN, who then fell for one of the so-called publishing discounts with a "free ISBN" and wound up paying the publisher three or four dollars extra for every book they print (from now till the end of time, world without end).

VANITY PUBLISHERS INSIST ON DECIDING THE RETAIL PRICE

A vanity publisher's profit comes from the books the author buys to either give away to family and friends or to sell to the reading public. For that reason, vanity publishers insist on deciding the retail price. They will set the price unreasonably high and then offer authors a whopping 50% discount to buy their own book. Sounds great, doesn't it? Who doesn't love a half-off sale?

Here's the catch: the higher the retail price, the more the authors pay for their own book. The more the author pays, the more the vanity publisher makes on printing. It's all about the money. The problem is, it's *your* money.

These bottom-feeders will charge the author $8 to print a $16 book (which should be priced at $12). They will then print it at Lightning Source for less than $3. Still have your calculator handy? They make five bucks a pop on every book.

HOW DO I DECIDE THE PROPER RETAIL PRICE FOR MY BOOK?

First you must find a publisher who will let you set the retail price. Then go to a bookstore and look at books similar in genre and size to yours. Stay in the same price range. Bookstores will price the book with their own label, but will usually stay near the price you suggest.

MAY I SUGGEST A CHECKUP FROM THE NECK UP?

If you see the words "assign" or "unique ISBN" in a publishing package, run, don't walk to the nearest online exit, and don't ever go back to that website. If you do, you will lose. If you are still considering going with an assigned ISBN and the publisher who offers it, may I suggest a checkup from the neck up?

Buy your own ISBN from www.bowker.com, the official dispenser of ISBNs in the U.S. You can buy one for $125 or ten for $295 (sometimes on sale for $275). You don't need to buy a barcode, because cover designers will provide the $25 barcode (usually included in their fee).

Because of the growing number of self-published authors buying their own ISBNs, R.R. Bowker has entered into agreements with twelve publishers who are designated as Bowker partners. They can submit official ISBN applications on behalf of self-published authors. They are Aardvark, Bethany Press, Expressio, FilmMasters, Instantpublisher.com, Lulu.com, PPC Books, Publisher Services, RJ Communications (selfpublishing.com), RKD Press, Signature Books, and WordClay.

If you did not buy your ISBN(s) directly from Bowker or one of these designated partners, you do *not* own the ISBN and are *not* a self-publisher. Be careful. If you buy through one of these official Bowker partners, check website details before you proceed. Some may offer other services or programs that include the publisher's ISBN and not yours.

Most true self-publishing companies/facilitators will insist you own the ISBN (Bethany Press/Believers Press, selfpublishing.com, and Morris Publishing among them).

If you plan more than one book, you might consider buying a block of ten. I bought ten initially and quickly needed more. This book will utilize two ISBNs (one for the paper version and one for the e-book version).

You will also want your book listed in Bowker Books in Print. After your book is published, call 877-310-7333, and they will walk you through the process, no charge.

WHAT IF I LIVE OUTSIDE THE U.S. OR CANADA?

British authors can go to http://www.isbn.nielsenbook. co.uk/controller.php?page=123. In the UK, single ISBNs are not available; you must buy ten ISBNs (107£). On the positive side, just the act of applying for an ISBN from Nielsen gets UK books listed with amazon.co.uk and Waterstones online booksellers.

New Zealand authors can obtain ISBNs (minimum of ten, but free) from the National Library of New Zealand at http://www.natlib.govt.nz/isbn-application.

Australian authors can apply for ISBNs at http://www.thorpe.com.au/en-AU. A single ISBN in Australia is only $40 AUS and a block of ten is a very reasonable $80 AUS.

For a complete list of ISBN agencies around the world (from Afghanistan to Zimbabwe), go to: http://isbn-information.com/isbn-agency.html. You can also Google "ISBN agency [your country]" to save time. You must buy ISBNs from the ISBN agency in the country where you reside.

QUESTION: What if a major publisher like Random House wants to publish my book?

ANSWER: They will own the ISBN, they will be the publisher of record, they will pay for everything, and they will make most of the money on your book. That's okay. You will make money, too, and maybe, just maybe, you will wind up on television talking about your best-seller book.

(While you are waiting to hear from Random House and the television networks, plan on self-publishing.)

SPEAKING OF EDITING . . .

Okay, we haven't talked about editing, but we need to, because it is kind of important.

CHAPTER 4

EDITING IS A MUST

Vanity publishers, as a rule, never include editing in any of their publishing packages (and they seldom come out and tell you that little fact). And most of these "editing not included" packages include that unique assigned ISBN. Remember, as a self-publisher, you want your own ISBN, not an assigned one.

Editing will add several hundred dollars to your overall publishing cost, but is money well spent.

IF YOU DON'T EDIT, DON'T PUBLISH

Editing will cost anywhere from a penny a word for a simple grammatical or mechanical edit, to a nickel a word and up for a thorough, comprehensive edit. The former deals with punctuation, grammar, and spelling; the latter deals with sentence structure, flow, and everything essential to make your book a good read. Bottom line: if you don't get at least a basic grammatical edit, don't publish.

If you can't afford editing, wait until you have the money. You are looking at $300 to $1500 to edit a 30,000-word book (about 150 pages).

HOW CAN YOU DETERMINE THE LEVEL OF EDITING YOU NEED?

Any credible editor will give you a free sample of their editing skills (usually around five hundred words) and suggest the editing level you should consider. It is worth an editor's time to do a sample edit to get your business.

SOME LITERARY AGENTS WILL DO CONSIDERABLE EDITING

If you are looking for a literary agent and a traditional publishing contract, you should think about polishing your book proposal and manuscript with at least a basic edit. If you are fortunate enough to find a literary agent who wants to represent you, he may help with editing. Some literary agents will do considerable editing to make your proposal and manuscript more appealing to prospective publishers.

Always check out any editor you are considering. If you find it difficult to get firm pricing from an editor, keep looking. True self-publishing companies/facilitators can refer you to reliable editing services.

A basic (mechanical) edit that corrects, for example, typos, misspellings, syntax, capitalization, and subject/ verb agreement, can cost .01 to .025 cents a word. A more substantive edit will run you .03 to .05 cents per word and includes things like organization and sentence structure (making for smooth, fun reading). A full or comprehensive edit can cost .06 to .08 per word or more and includes all the other levels, plus a thorough critique of your manuscript.

IT WILL STILL BE YOUR WRITING, JUST NEW AND IMPROVED

A good editor always tries to keep the author's style and voice as much as possible. It will still be your writing, just new and improved. Editors use different terms like *line-editing*, *copy editing*, *content editing*, and *proofreading*, but most think in terms of the three levels of editing described above. Proofreading is usually done after printing the galley proof (actual copy) to make sure everything is just right before going to press.

Other editors may charge by the page from $3.75 to $5.00 per page, based on a 250-word page (a typical page in Word, double-spaced). The numbers work out about the same as a per-word charge. Some editors offer a per-hour charge.

IF YOU CAN'T WRITE AT ALL

If your writing is average to above average (because you have decent grammar skills), you might get by with a basic edit. If your writing needs help, a more substantive edit would be good. If you can't write at all, but have a great story to tell, you might consider a ghost writer. They, too, will give you a sample with pricing (and, often, can edit as they rewrite from your notes and suggestions).

Along with the price, the experience and credentials of the prospective editor are important as well. Most professional book editors follow the Chicago Manual of Style (CMS). There are other style guides (some editors use MLA, Modern Language Association), but if you meet any alleged editor who is not at least familiar with the Chicago Manual of Style, politely excuse yourself from further contact. This person is not a book editor.

Information on the correct use of numbers in manuscripts and a ton of information about proper writing and grammar is available at The Purdue Online Writing Lab at http://owl.english.purdue.edu/owl/resource/551/01. Use the site map and search function on the Owl site to answer any question about writing.

Christian authors need to be familiar with the proper abbreviations of the books of the Bible listed here: http://hbl.gcc.edu/abbreviationsCHICAGO.htm.

Many online self-publishing companies offer an *editorial analysis*. Most of these analyses are offered by vanity publishers, which makes them suspect at the outset. They lead inexperienced authors to think their whole manuscript will be edited for a small fee. It won't. Selfpublishing.com has a reliable editorial analysis.

THEY WILL PRINT IT, MISSPELLED WORDS AND ALL

Never confuse an editorial analysis with a full manuscript edit. The analysis will cover only eight to ten pages. Personally, I wouldn't use most vanity publishers' editorial analysis, because they won't mind if you don't edit your book. They will print it, misspelled words and all. I wouldn't trust a vanity publisher's alleged editing experts either. There are exceptions, but not many.

My friend, James, paid a vanity publisher $900 to edit his 120-page book. I have a copy and found multiple typos on every page (including misspelled words, improper spacing, and absurd punctuation).

Some offer editing by the hour. I would only consider hourly editing if I personally knew the editor or knew someone who used the editor and was very satisfied with the price and quality of the work. Most hourly editors will set a limit or cap they will charge per project.

LIKE A BIG ZIT ON THE END OF YOUR NOSE

Here I go again (in case you missed it the first time): if you don't edit your book, *don't publish it.* An unedited book will stick out like a big zit on the end of your nose, even to a casual reader. The average bookstore manager will notice an unedited book even quicker and won't consider it for shelf space. Yes, you *can* get your book on the shelf here and there if it is professionally produced and doesn't have a vanity publisher's name or logo.

Another reason bookstores avoid vanity press books is because they are non-returnable. If a book doesn't sell, they want their money back, no questions asked. They will, at times, stock non-returnable books if they believe they will sell. On the downside, 84% of books in large US bookstores sell two copies or less each year, according to experienced bookstore managers. Not per month—*per year.* Only 2% sell 10 or more copies in a year.

BACK IN THE OLDEN DAYS

I know the reading skills of the average person are not what they were forty years ago (back in the olden days when we still taught a little grammar in our public schools). Newspapers, not too long ago, were written on an eighth-grade reading level. Today they are written so the average fifth-grader can muddle through the articles in social studies class. People who like books, however, are better readers on average. They will notice typos.

A professional book editor will provide insight and suggestions that will make your book "the best it can be" and will ensure that it conforms to modern publishing industry standards. Your old English teacher may be adept at correcting typos and misspellings, but a good editor will make suggestions your former teacher would never think of. Editors have a way of putting themselves in a reader's shoes.

Having said that, if all you want is someone to find all the typos, an English teacher might do the trick and save you money. Just keep in mind—if they don't charge you because, "you were such a nice student," it could take forever.

Patricia Fry wrote an article explaining why using your former English teacher might not be the best idea. Read it at:

http://www.matilijapress.com/publishingblog/?p=2269. If you still need convincing, read another article by Mark Levine: http://www.book-editing.com/editing-articles/editing-self-publishing.html.

IT COULD BECOME A LIFE-LONG RELATIONSHIP

Investigate prospective editors thoroughly. Ask for references from other authors who have used their editing service. If an editor is reluctant to supply author references, you should keep looking until you find one you are comfortable with. It could become a life-long relationship. If your book sells, you will want to write another one. That will be good news to your favorite editor. Like literary agents, editors are always looking for long-term partnerships with promising writers.

While editing is important, good cover design is imperative. No one will read your professionally edited book if the cover fails to get their attention. Whoever said, "You can't judge by its cover," was probably not an author, a publisher, or a bookseller.

CHAPTER 5
YOU *CAN* JUDGE A BOOK BY ITS COVER

The old adage "You can't judge a book by its cover" may or may not be true, but one thing is certain: the cover is the first thing someone sees and it better be eye-catching and alluring enough to tempt a prospective buyer to open your book and read a little.

Your book cover is the litmus test of first impressions. I admit, I have met a few people who made a bad first impression but later turned out to be wonderful people and good friends. But when it comes to books, you can't afford a cover that makes a bad first impression, because you won't get a second chance.

Have you heard of the "two-second rule"? If someone picks up your book, you have about two seconds to lure them into cracking it open, glancing through it, and (hopefully) buying it. It should be a *love at first sight* experience.

Here is the typical order:

1. Look at the cover (two-second clock starts).

2. Look at the back cover (*if* the front grabs you).

3. Open the book (*if* the back cover reels you in).

4. Decide to buy it and make you rich and famous.

That whole episode will take less than sixty seconds.

I recently learned first-hand how important a good cover design can be when I visited one of my favorite Christian bookstores in Florida. Bo Raulerson, thirty-five-year owner of Bartow Christian Bookstore, told me he believes covers sell more books than anything else.

Michael Hyatt, former CEO of Thomas Nelson Publishers, wrote an excellent article titled "Four Strategies for Creating Titles That Jump Off the Page."[3] After suggesting the first thing readers look at is the title, he says great titles do at least one of the following: "make a *promise*, create *intrigue*, identify a *need*, or simply state the *content*."[4]

One of the best-kept secrets in publishing is Art Bookbindery Inc. They printed my latest book. If you print with them (at least one hundred copies), your cover design and interior layout are free. I supplied the cover image and they did the rest. The cover is exceptional and the book is top quality. Unlike most digital printers, the more you print with Art Bookbindery, the cheaper it gets.

Readers are very selective. A really great book with a so-so cover will not spark attention. On the other hand, if you are a best-selling author, no one will care about the cover. Fans of your writing will order your new book before it prints.

WAIT UNTIL YOU CAN AFFORD IT

Unfortunately, most writers don't have a following or national face recognition, so everything about a debut book is important, including the cover. Just like editing: if you don't have funds to pay a professional designer to make your cover shine, wait until you can afford it. Some things you can cut corners on, but not editing and certainly not cover design.

The back cover is as important as the front. If the front cover tempts someone to read the back, it should pull them along and fill their minds with subliminal "buy me" messages. The front and back should also tell readers what is inside the book. Too often, the book cover doesn't reflect the content. If the prospective buyer is prompted to open the book, they will notice right away if the content is not what the cover suggests, and "plop"— the book goes back on the shelf.

I CAN SHOW YOU BETTER THAN I CAN TELL YOU

The front cover of a book should echo the tried and true sales pitch, "I can show you better than I can tell you." Your cover should *show* the reader what the book is about. Otherwise, you will be guilty of the old car salesman's "bait and switch" tactic. Unlike the pesky car salesman, you won't be there to resell them on the product.

WHY, AGAIN, IS THE BACK COVER IMPORTANT?

The back cover should continue to draw the reader into reading and buying. By the way, the average bookstore patron will drop $20 each visit without hesitation. A good cover should earn you a piece of that.

WHAT SHOULD I PUT ON THE BACK COVER?

The back cover content goes into a little more detail as to what the book is about. It should be a small taste, a tidbit sample of what is inside. One of my teacher friends at school looked at the back of my last book and said, "I want this; how much is it?" The back content sold her.

WHAT ELSE GOES ON THE BACK?

You do. A picture is still worth a thousand words, but don't use a grainy photo someone took of you on their cell phone. If you don't have a good head shot of yourself, go to a photographer and spend $60 for a decent facsimile of your beautiful smile. PS: a mug shot is not appropriate, and don't use a ten-year-old photo when you know you haven't looked that good for a while. You do plan on at least a few book signings, don't you? An old picture makes you look a little dishonest. So you have a few wrinkles—who cares? I decided years ago that my opinion of myself has nothing to do with what anyone else thinks of me.

Lastly, a brief bio should tell why you are qualified to write such a book, or why you felt a burden to write. Like the rest of the back cover content, keep the bio short and sweet. Few people read every word on the back of any book. As I like to say, *Don't be too general, just give me the details.* Just kidding; keep it short and to the point. Too many details will cause readers to zone out.

Time to change gears. How long has it been since someone tried to mislead you? Chances are, if you have been to a vanity publisher's website lately, it was more recent than you think.

CHAPTER 6
THE BIG FIB

It is time to talk about the good, bad, and ugly practices of vanity/indie publishers. I don't want to come right and say they lie, so I'll just suggest many vanity publishers are often less than forthright. I'm not suggesting everyone who works for a vanity publisher is dishonest. Most are nice folks just trying to make a living, but they are obligated to follow company guidelines that would make it difficult for me to work for one of these publishers.

Some folks believe if you tell a lie often enough, loud enough, and long enough, people will believe it. Vanity publishers, one and all, are doing just that when they say, "You retain all the rights to your book." Several other spins dovetail off that assertion. Let's look at the claim and break it down.

Here is a direct quote from an unnamed vanity publisher's website: "As a self-publisher, you own all rights to your book."

You don't own *all* the rights; I don't care what they say. They have repeated the myth so long, they seem to believe it themselves. Don't blame the youthful sales people you talk to. They read from a script and answer questions from the in-house reference guide covering every possible objection authors may bring up. Some of what we discuss will be familiar, but, at the risk of repeating myself, you really need to understand the following facts:

> *Fact #1: You don't own the publishing rights if you have an "assigned" ISBN, and the publisher will make as much money as you on every book sold (remember, they haven't invested a dime—you paid for everything). Buy your own ISBN and kick that vanity publisher to the curb. They will stop bothering you if you insist and keep insisting on using your own ISBN.*

> *Fact #2: You won't own or retain any rights to the digital files for your book. The few vanity publishers that do offer files will charge a hefty fee (true self-publishing companies/facilitators will provide files at a reasonable cost).*

> *Fact #3: You probably won't contractually own the rights to the cover design or the interior layout.*

In other words, you won't own diddly.

THEY DON'T MIND IF YOU LEAVE

There is at least one good thing vanity publishers do. They offer contracts that are "non-exclusive," which means you can cancel the contract any time (usually with a written, thirty-day notice). They don't mind if you leave—they made all their money up front.

There is one titanic drawback: you can only take your raw manuscript with you. The vanity publisher owns everything else. You will have to start from scratch with a new title, new cover design, new interior layout, and a new ISBN (now you're talking!). Consider that wonderful experience with a vanity publisher to be a dry run and an expensive lesson learned. Start over with your own ISBN. Forgive me; I'm starting to sound like a nag. I *am* a nag—buy your own ISBN!

Those few publishers that allow you to or insist you provide your own ISBN won't own anything but the money you paid to get your book in print. They will charge reasonable fees for digital copies of high-resolution front and back cover images and the interior layout. You can take those files and turn them into an e-book for Amazon's Kindle, Barnes and Noble's Nook, and every other online e-book seller. As a true self-publisher with your own ISBN, you will own all the rights, including the publishing rights.

WE WILL PUBLISH YOUR BOOK FOR FREE

Like pick-pockets who believe in practicing to hone their skills, vanity publishers are constantly coming up with new tricks and ruses to extract money from vulnerable authors. One approach in some vanity publishers' playbook starts with the claim, "We will publish your book for free." They insist they will pay for everything: the cover design, the (unedited) interior layout, and the ISBN (assigned of course). As to the "publish for free" claim, remember, "There is no such thing as a free lunch."

Here's the catch: they don't charge for anything during the process, just as they promised. All you have to do is agree beforehand (with your credit card number) to buy the first two thousand copies hot off the press. Never fear, they will give you that familiar 50% author discount. Because *they know the market* (yeah, right), they will set the retail price (usually pretty high).

Suppose the retail price for your book is $14.99. With that breathtaking half-off discount, you can buy those first two thousand books for just $7.50 each. That comes to $15,000 you will pay for that "free" book. What a deal. Are you hyperventilating yet?

WAKE UP AND SMELL THE INK

I published my last book with a professionally designed cover, expert typesetting (interior layout), and a skilled edit. Including shipping costs, I had three hundred books delivered to my door for a grand total of $2100. Had I ordered two thousand books initially, my total cost would have been around $4,000. What do you think that "publish for free" guy did with the other $11,000 you paid? Wake up and smell the ink. He's picking out custom cabinets for his new kitchen and his wife thanks you for your generosity (and her new wardrobe).

First of all, you don't need two thousand books. Two to three hundred will do to start. You can always order more books at a reasonable reprint cost (if you own the ISBN). You don't want fifteen boxes of books in your garage succumbing to heat, cold, and moisture, with covers curling up like elbow macaroni.

Another common ploy is the claim, "We are a traditional publisher." They hope you don't really know how a traditional publisher operates. *If* an agent responded to your well-crafted query letter and asked for a book proposal, and *if* the agent managed to sell one of the big boys on publishing your book, and *if* you signed a contract with that traditional publisher, several good things will happen (none of which will cost you a dime).

WILL IT MAKE US MONEY?

You will probably get at least a small advance in the four-figure range (which will be deducted from your future royalty checks). They will fully edit and tweak your manuscript until it has the best chance to make a profit. Did I say, *profit?*

You need to understand something. Traditional publishers don't care if a book is good. The only question they ask is, *Will it make us money?* Don't be offended; you will make money, as well—maybe lots of money.

On the down side, it could take a year for an agent to sell your manuscript, and another year or two, for your book to hit bookshelves nationwide. On the up side, when it does, people will buy it.

Here is another little secret vanity publishers posing as traditional publishers don't want you to know: traditional publishers never charge anything to publish and distribute your book. Your wallet and your credit cards can gather dust for all they care. The publisher decided your book was a money-maker or they would not have offered you a contract.

WHAT ARE YOU SAYING, TED?

If any publisher asks for money up front, they are not, I repeat, are not a traditional publisher. One alleged traditional publisher charges the author several thousand dollars, while promising to spend thousands more to market and sell the book. If you buy into that tall tale, I have a frost-free oven I'd like to sell you. Hey, it really works—I've never seen one ice crystal on it.

That is not how traditional publishers operate. It *is* how subsidy publishers function. It is called *co-publishing* or *co-op* or *joint-venture* publishing. The publisher "partners" with the author and they invest together (supposedly). I would need a thorough investigation and lots of references before signing with a subsidy publisher. Even with a squeaky-clean report, I probably still wouldn't do it. You should totally ignore any alleged traditional publisher that asks for money. They are either confused about what they really are or intentionally dishonest.

I wouldn't try to scare you, but a friend who owns his own publishing company told me someone came to him for help, having spent just over $100,000 with a so-called subsidy publisher. Sales were scant. The author lost his shirt. The publisher did great. Maybe I *am* trying to scare you. Is it working?

AVAILABLE TO 25,000 BOOKSTORES NATIONWIDE

The mistruths (fibs) keep coming. Here is one of my favorites: "We have a great distribution network that will make your book available to 25,000 bookstores nationwide." *Wow! Really? Where do I sign?* Slow your roll, partner. Read between the lines. They don't say your book will be on bookshelves because they know it won't. It *will* be in the Ingram database 25,000 bookstores use to order your book if someone walks in and asks for it. Until then, it languishes in an invisible databank. "Distribution" or "available" means listing in Ingram's database, nothing more.

If a publisher you are considering says, "We have distribution," and, "Your book will be available to 25,000 bookstores nationwide," ask, *Does that mean you have sales people who will go to Barnes and Noble's corporate office and personally pitch my book to get them to order it and put it on the shelf?* The answer will always be a sheepish *no*—after a flurry of verbal tap-dancing.

FINDING AN HONEST PUBLISHER

At a given point, you will face the daunting task of finding an honest publisher. They are a little harder to detect, but your personally-owned ISBN is a magnet that will attract true self-publishing facilitators and, at the same time, repel vanity gnats.

CHAPTER 7

NEEDLE IN A
HAYSTACK

After several years of writing and re-writing, a friend
felt comfortable with her manuscript. "Now what?" she
asked.

Before self-publishing my first book, I determined
to answer that question and spent the better part of a
year exploring the publishing industry and the process of
getting a book in print. I learned more than I anticipated,
including a number of pitfalls and snags to avoid at all
costs.

To put it bluntly, safely publishing a book requires
tip-toeing through a virtual financial minefield to find
the proverbial needle in a haystack—*a true self-publishing
facilitator.* If you don't know what you are doing, some
unscrupulous vanity publisher will detonate your
checkbook (but only after they have drained your bank
account).

Again, I use the term *facilitator,* because these
companies help you become a self-publisher. Technically,
they are not self-publishing companies; they are self-
publishing facilitators.

Major publishers like Random House, Simon &

Schuster, or Thomas J. Nelson will not be interested in your manuscript unless your name is Hillary Clinton, Ann Coulter, or Billy Graham. The challenge is finding a publisher who is willing to work with you to produce a quality self-published book at a fair price.

EASIER THAN YOU THINK

Finding such a publisher is easier than you think. It is a simple matter of finding one that will let you use your own ISBN. My personal experience with RJ Communications and Art Bookbindery puts both at the top of my personal list of true self-publishing facilitators.

A few other companies will allow you to use your ISBN and set the retail price for your book, including Bethany Press, Bookmasters, and Morris Publishing. I emailed each and those listed responded rather quickly with an okay to use my own ISBN (and they don't hide that fact from authors). There are others that let you use your own ISBN, but they make it difficult to find ISBN information, and they usually offer a free, assigned ISBN as an option.

Be sure to investigate each publisher thoroughly before you decide. If any is reluctant to answer your questions quickly and candidly, or don't make it obvious that authors can use their own ISBN, walk away. If you email me about a publisher you are considering, I will give you my honest—yes or no—opinion.

Two other places to find candid publisher reviews are Predators & Editors (http://pred-ed.com/), and the Absolute Write Water Cooler (http://www.absolutewrite.

com/forums/).

Getting answers to a few basic questions will enable you to join forces with a publisher you can trust to produce your book professionally and economically.

ARE YOU A PUBLISHER WHO WILL . . .

1. let me use my own ISBN?

2. show all prices up front?

3. gladly provide marketing resources and advice?

4. be accessible by phone, toll free, anytime I have a question during the publishing process?

5. provide files for my cover and content at a reasonable price?

6. let me set the retail price for my book?

7. send a proof of my book for final inspection and corrections before going to press?

8. not require me to sign a contract?

If you ask a prospective publisher these questions and get instant answers without stone walling, you are probably safe going with that publisher. Of course, you should compare prices with other publishers, but the best price is not always the best deal. Take your time and choose wisely.

Once you find a publisher you are comfortable with, they will walk you through each step. Before you know it, your manuscript will be on its way to the printer. Speaking of printers. . .

CHAPTER 8

ALL PRINTERS ARE NOT CREATED EQUAL

Editing is finished, the cover is beautiful, the interior content is neatly laid out, and you made a few corrections after you (and a couple of your friends) read and re-read your galley proof (an actual paper copy of your printed book). If you can afford the penny-per-word a proofreader charges to make one last check of your book, that would be a good thing. If you are out of extra money, go ahead and pay for printing and shipping and push that submit button. In a few days, the presses will roll. You are now a few short weeks from opening that first box of books. It's a rush.

Worried about typos you missed? No book is perfect. You can still make minor corrections (at a small cost) even after the first print run.

CAN I GO TO A LOCAL MOM-AND-POP PRINTER TO GET MY BOOK PRINTED?

There are book printers and there is every other kind of printer. Book printers print books and not much else. Other printers print everything else and, occasionally, try book printing. Local print shops fall into the latter category.

Have you ever seen a paperback book with the pages falling out? I'm reading one right now. If it wasn't one of my favorites, I would throw it away. The problem is with the binding that holds the book together. Most complaints about self-published paperback books have to do with inferior binding.

AGAINST THE GRAIN

When paper is manufactured, it comes out of the paper-making machine in a continuous strip ranging from a few inches wide to a few feet. Visualize the spinning paper rolls of a newspaper grinding out the daily edition. The grain of the paper flows lengthwise. Take a piece of print paper and fold it in the middle from top to bottom. You will notice a nice, clean, vertical crease. But if you fold it side to side, across the middle, the crease will be a bit rough, because you are folding against the grain.

Paper is half the expense of printing a book. A local printer will be tempted to print and bind against the grain just to save money. A typical piece of printer paper measuring 8½ inches by 11 inches, cut in half, will produce two pages measuring 5½ by 8½ inches, the perfect size page for a book. The problem is, if you do that, you might save some paper, but you will be binding that book against the grain. The pages will work loose in time.

Granted, a quality book bindery can produce a book that will stay together, even if the pages are bound against the grain, but professional book printers never bind against the grain. They won't chance it. Professional binding equipment can cost $750,000 to over $2,000,000. The print shop around the corner may boast about the $40,000 bindery they invested in, but if they bind a book against the grain to save money, the pages will, sooner rather than later, begin to fall out. Even binding with the grain, a cheaper bindery may not guarantee a durable book.

SHE HAD TO REFUND EVERY DOLLAR

The friend I mentioned, who owns his own publishing company and print facility, told me the story of a woman who came to him in tears. She went with a local, hometown printer and every one of her two thousand books fell apart as soon as they were opened. The printer refused to refund her money. She had to return every dollar for books already sold.

I'm not knocking local print shops; most just don't have the right equipment to bind books. Use your own judgment.

THE BASIC DIFFERENCE IS TONER VERSUS INK

What is the difference between digital printing and offset printing?

The basic difference is toner versus ink. Although professional digital print equipment costs a lot more than a home laser printer, the print process is similar.

Digital printers use toner and heat to produce books. Do you recall feeling warm pages the last time you printed several copies on a laser printer? Heat is necessary to fuse the print toner to the paper. The heat draws moisture from the paper and the pages need a few hours after printing to recapture most (but not all) of the natural moisture.

Offset presses use ink and don't require heat to bond the print with the paper, so the finished product is higher quality because the paper doesn't go through a drying and moisture-recuperating process.

Nowadays, digital printing is nearly as good as offset printing as far as looks go. Only a pro can tell the difference. Bookstores still prefer offset printed books.

THE MORE YOU PRINT, THE CHEAPER IT GETS

The real advantage to offset printing is the cost per book. With digital printing, the print price never goes down. With offset printing, the more you print, the cheaper it gets. At $3 per book for a 150-page paperback, 10,000 digitally-printed books would cost $30,000. You can offset print 10,000 copies of the same book for about a dollar each.

Digital printing should work fine for the average author, because you only need a few hundred books to start with. On the other hand, if someone wants to buy two thousand copies of your book, offset is the way to go.

All commercial publishers use offset printing, because they print anywhere from five thousand to one million books per print run. There are only five or six offset printers in America large enough to accommodate traditional publishers' volume requirements. Smaller offset printers handle runs as few as five hundred copies.

At the end of the day, you want your books professionally printed, whether digital or offset. Proper binding will ensure against refunding books that didn't hold up. I am reminded of the guy who said, *I was reading a book on obsolescence, but I couldn't finish because it fell apart.*

Speaking of digital printing, have you ever heard of a company called Lightning Source?

CHAPTER 9

LIGHTNING SOURCE STRIKES

If you have never heard of Lightning Source, I'm not surprised. They are the largest digital printing company on Earth but they only print books for publishers (over 24,000 of them). They won't deal with you as an author unless you own the ISBN. ISBN ownership makes you a publisher.

Have you ever wondered what happens when someone orders a book from an online bookstore like Barnes & Noble? Once a customer hits the *Buy Now* button, the order goes to Lightning Source in La Vergne, Tennessee. The file number for that book is entered into the printer's computer and forty-five seconds later, the finished book rolls out the other end, ready to ship. Lightning Source digitally stores over seven million titles and adds thousands of new titles each month.

POD HAS REVOLUTIONIZED THE BOOK INDUSTRY

It is called Print On Demand (POD). POD has revolutionized the book industry. Lightning Source works behind the scenes, fulfilling online book orders for the overwhelming majority of small, medium, and major publishers around the world. Books are printed one at a time or in small bulk orders, depending on how many a customer wants.

Here is the neat part: Lightning Source and Ingram Book Company are owned by the same parent company, Ingram Content Group. Ingram Book Company is the largest wholesale book distributor in the world and is less than three blocks down the street from Lightning Source. Lightning Source prints it, someone runs it down the street, and Ingram ships it out within twenty-four hours. When you walk into any bookstore and ask about a book you can't find on the shelf, the clerk will pull up Ingram's database, order the book, and have it delivered to your house within days after Lightning Source prints it.

Like I said, as an author you can't go to Lightning Source to print your books. As a self-published author with your own ISBN, you can. You will have to provide print-ready files for your book, but if you use the right self-publisher, you can buy those files.

If you don't want to get into preparing print-ready files (I don't and won't), you can pay a nominal fee and the publisher you use can get your book listed with Ingram, making it available with every Internet bookseller.

Because Lightning Source has facilities all over the world, your book will be available in America, England, Europe, Asia, and just about everywhere in between. You can buy my latest book online in England for 7.87£ (3.29£ for Kindle e-book). It is a bit mind-boggling what the Internet has done to enhance business around the world.

WHEN YOU OWN THE ISBN, YOU ARE THE PUBLISHER

To repeat: when you own the ISBN, you are not just a self-publisher, you are the publisher. Even though you are an individual, with ISBN ownership, LS sees no difference between you and an established publishing company. That is another secret vanity publishers don't want you to know—but you don't have to get that involved.

As I said, publishers that let you use your own ISBN can get your book listed online at Amazon, Barnes & Noble, and every other Internet bookseller for a small fee (usually under $100), and then less than twenty dollars a year to keep it active.

You don't need to understand all the intricate details about how print on demand works. Just know it will work for you as an author/publisher.

You can start your own publishing company if you choose, or you can skip that step. I started JC Publishers LLC in Florida for $125. An LLC is designated by most states as a company that can "conduct any and all business." I can sell a book one day and a pound of shrimp the next. I don't sell shrimp, but I could.

It's interesting when the phone rings at my house. JC Publishers sounds like a big outfit, especially when you see the size of my website. When I answer the phone, some folks pause, because they expected a secretary to say, "JC Publishers, how may I direct your call?"

I just say, "Hello, this is Ted."

I'm just one man doing a three-man job. You don't

need employees to start an LLC.

You can start your own publishing company or you can operate as a book-at-a-time, unincorporated self-publisher.

Enough about business. Let's talk book size. Page count is important—but with books, bigger is not always better.

CHAPTER 10
HOW BIG SHOULD MY BOOK BE?

I often ask new authors about the word-count for the manuscript they are working on. With a self-assured smile, one writer said confidently, "250,000 words so far." That is already a 1000-page book no one will buy, but not because the price will be too high. People don't typically like books that lengthy.

I hear you objecting, "What about *Harry Potter*?" When you become a famous author, you can write big books and your fans will buy and read them. When it comes to books for the general public, smaller is better. The first Harry Potter book was only 320 pages.

Do you remember the friend I talked about earlier who wrote a book on dreams and heard from a traditional publisher? The owner said he learned over the last few years that the average reader prefers a book to be no more than 150 to 180 pages. I'm not sure if it has to do with the busy lifestyles we enjoy (or endure), or the fact that the average person wants everything to be quick, short, and sweet. Of course, that was only one publisher's opinion.

He went on to say the average woman likes a book that will fit neatly into her purse and a man wants a book that won't take up too much room in his briefcase or in the compact travel bag he stuffs in the overhead bin as he jets hither and yon. Pre-POD print masters will insist that a real book must be at least 260 pages; any less and it's just a pamphlet. Times are changing. People want smaller books. When I buy a book, I expect it to get to the point and tell me what I want to know without a bunch of excess verbiage.

IT TOOK TOO LONG TO GET TO THE POINT

I have read three hundred-page books that could have been a hundred pages shorter. It was obvious the author fluffed it up to increase page count. Those books bore me before I get too far along. I sometimes ask a friend to read a book first to get her thoughts. More often than not, she will say, "I just couldn't get into it. It took too long to get to the point."

> *A sentence should contain no unnecessary words, a paragraph no unnecessary sentences, for the same reason that a drawing should have no unnecessary lines and a machine no unnecessary parts.*

(WILLIAM STRUNK, JR., THE ELEMENTS OF STYLE, 1918)

Our collective attention spans are shrinking by the day. We all seem to be impacted by time crunches and deadlines. At this point in my life, I don't even want to invest two hours in a movie on television. I usually fall asleep and wonder how it ended. I would rather watch a one-hour reality show about something that really interests me. If it doesn't keep my attention, I'll reach for the remote.

What were we talking about? Oh, yes, book size.

A 125-page book will be about 30,000 words. My latest book was 164 pages (44,000 words), and this one will be about 25,000 words (100 pages). The average novel is 90,000 to 110,000 words (300–400 pages).

Speaking of novels, if you send a query letter and give a word count for your debut novel of 150,000 words or more, the agent will hit the delete button before reading another line. Stay under the 100,000-word limit until you are famous. It costs publishers money to print those big books. They shy away unless your name is Stephen King.

CAN I TELL HOW BIG MY FINISHED BOOK WILL BE, BASED ON THE NUMBER OF MANUSCRIPT PAGES?

Yes, you can. Here is one rule of thumb: one page in Word, double-spaced (editors prefer double-spaced) in 12-point Courier New font, equals about $1\frac{1}{4}$ pages in a $5\frac{1}{2}$ by $8\frac{1}{2}$ inch paperback. In other words, if your double-spaced manuscript in Word is a hundred pages, your printed book will be about 125 pages. It's not an exact science but it gives you a rough idea of the final page count. Or, you could divide your total word count by 250 (average number of words on a page).

A GOOD AUTHOR WRITES AND THEN CUTS AND GUTS

If your current manuscript has a gazillion words, don't panic. Remember: a good author writes and then cuts and guts. There will be lots of literary blood. If you can eliminate any sentence in a paragraph without losing the meaning of that paragraph, you don't need that sentence.

You can also cut the word *that* from almost every sentence without losing your thought. While you are at it, eliminate as many words ending in *ly* as you can. These are ~~usually~~ adverbs you can do without (unless you are writing fiction).

Don't stop now. Grit your teeth and gut your book of most passive sentences. Instead of, "I was told by the doctor ~~that~~ [cut the word *that*] I needed surgery," write, "The doctor said I needed surgery."

One of my favorite resources for writing tips is Audrey Owen's Website: http://www.writershelper.com/writingtips.html.

If you are convinced your seven hundred-page book has to stand its ground as is, you might think about making it a three-book series at 235 pages each. If you don't, I'll say it again: *not many will want to read your mega-page fluff ball.*

HOW LONG SHOULD A CHAPTER BE?

That's like asking, "How long should a board be?" There is no set rule. The answer is, *However long it needs to be to do the job.* Consider works of fiction first. The average novel is 90,000 words with 20 to 40 chapters. Taking the average of 250 words per page, that works out to 2000 to 4500 words per chapter (or 8 to 18 pages per chapter). Again, there are no set rules. By the way, the average adult reads about 250 words per minute. The average middle school student reads about 150 words per minute.

THINGS TO CONSIDER:

1. The bedtime reader likes to read a single chapter in a favorite book before bedtime. Ten to twenty-page chapters are perfect.

2. The lunchtime reader has a time limit. Five-page chapters are great.

3. The morning commuter on the train has more time. Any length will suffice.

4. Many like to read in ten to fifteen minute spurts; others, an hour or more at a time.

Conclusion: more breaks in a story are less irritating than fewer breaks. Translation: shorter chapters are better than longer chapters.

The average reader today has become a skimmer thanks to the Internet. Five pages per chapter appeal to the skimmer and the Internet is birthing more skimmers by the hour. (James Patterson's novels have chapters averaging 3 to 5 pages).

Holes, by Louis Sachar, is 47,000 words, 50 chapters, 940 words per chapter (4 pages).

Harry Potter and the Sorcerer's Stone, by J.K. Rowlings is 77,000 words, 17 chapters, 4559 words per chapter (18 pages).

The Hunger Game, by Suzanne Collins is 99,750 words, 27 chapters, 3,700 words per chapter (14 pages).

As I said, there is no set number. A chapter should be long enough to cover the topic and short enough to keep it interesting. In non-fiction, shorter is better. Truth is stranger than fiction, but takes less time to tell the story. Non-fiction books are typically half to three-quarters the size of novels. No matter what your genre, don't cram words into a chapter to make it fit into a smaller format and don't fluff up your content just to make a chapter longer. Say what you want to say and "Gitter done." If you are writing a novel, you can still say what you want to say and get to the point—just do it with verbal images and enough emotion to touch the reader's heart as well as his mind.

Now it is time to switch gears. What if you don't want to self-publish, but would rather go straight to the pot of gold at the end of the traditional publishing rainbow? There is a very specific way to proceed and you must do it right to have a chance. First, you will need a literary agent...and rhino skin.

CHAPTER 11
DO I NEED A LITERARY AGENT?

If you self-publish your book, you won't need an agent. If you want to go for the gold and land a book deal, you will usually need the services of a professional literary agent.

Your chance of success may be slim, but your book could have potential. You have nothing to lose but the time and effort it takes to send out dozens of email and snail mail queries to agents. Experts say you should send five to ten queries at a time, then wait to hear back. Most agents are courteous and will email back the same day or shortly thereafter (usually with a polite, "It's not what we are looking for right now").

WHAT IS A LITERARY AGENT?

Literary agents represent literary works by authors (books). The dream of becoming a best-selling author requires getting a traditional publisher to buy your manuscript. Problem: they won't often entertain you because commercial publishers don't accept unsolicited manuscripts from authors. They primarily talk to agents.

Reputable agents know the publishers and their acquisition editors and which ones will be interested in the genre (subject) of your book. In other words, they have connections and you don't. For that reason alone, if you are a serious author, you should at least try to find representation. Notice I said *try.*

Be aware, there are unprincipled literary agents just as there are dishonest vanity publishers. They are not bonafide agents and I can show you how to spot them a mile away. True agents never ask for money. We'll talk more about that later in the chapter.

A BELL-RINGING QUERY LETTER

So how do I go about getting a real literary agent to take me on, Ted? First, get your rhino skin on and get ready for lots of rejections.

You need to carefully craft a query letter that will knock an agent's socks off. Understand at the outset, a query letter is the only thing an agent will read initially. They won't ask for proposals or manuscripts unless a query letter gets their attention. A query has one specific purpose: to get the agent to contact you. One of the best sources of information for writing a great query letter is: http://www.agentquery.com/writer_hq.aspx.

WHAT IS A QUERY LETTER?

It is a one-page document that has three basic elements: a *headline* or *teaser* (a one-sentence grabber or hook that rattles the agent's cage), a *synopsis* or overview (a 150-word mini-version of your 250-page manuscript), and a short *author bio* (your writing experience, if you have any, and what qualifies you to write this book, or why you wrote it).

SMALLER IS ALWAYS BETTER IN A QUERY

A query letter is never, ever, more than one page, written in 12-point font, single-spaced. If you have to reduce the font size and adjust the margins to get your letter to fit on one page, it is too big. Smaller is always better in a query.

Carefully address your letter to a specific agent by name. Never say, *Dear Sir* or *To whom it may concern* (there goes that delete button). Begin with a polite request that the agent consider your book. Include the word count and title of your book.

Close by thanking the agent for their time and conclude with your contact information: name, address, telephone number, and email address. Say you have a book proposal (non-fiction) or a completed manuscript (fiction) ready to send on request.

Each agent has strict guidelines to follow when you query, including the contact method. Most agents prefer email queries these days; a few still like snail mail. Do exactly what the agent specifies, nothing more and nothing less. *Don't send your query letter as an attachment* (agents won't open attachments). Embed it in the email. Then wait.

Many agents reply rather quickly, often the same day. A few won't reply at all, but only a few. Most will decline for one reason or another. That's why you need that rhino skin.

A few literary agents won't even consider you unless you already have one book published. (Sorry, self-published books don't qualify.) Look for agents who say they are open to receive queries from new or unpublished authors.

Charlotte Dillon hosts a great website on query letter guidelines and just about everything a writer needs to know in the area of query letters at http://www. charlottedillon.com/query.html.

WHAT IF AN AGENT REQUESTS A BOOK PROPOSAL?

It's time to break out the root beer, ginger ale, kickapoo juice, champagne, or whatever you prefer to celebrate with. Agents don't respond unless they think your book could be a winner. That's agent talk for *money, money, money.*

If an agent does call you, don't blow it by talking too much. They're not calling to offer you a contract . . . yet. The agent, more than anything else, will decide from the conversation whether they want to work with you. If an agent discovers a good writer, they anticipate a long-term agent/author relationship, but few agents want to work with difficult authors. If they decide, after a minute or two, you are an *EPR* (Extra Patience Required) or a *PIB* (Pain In the Buttocks), they will politely decline further contact.

Let the agent direct the conversation. If they say they would like to send you a contract, that is huge. Now it's really time for the bubbly. Agentquery.com goes into detail about what to do if an agent calls at http://www. agentquery.com/writer_or.aspx.

If an agent does respond to your query, it is common courtesy to let all the other agents you have queried know you have received a request for a proposal. That will prompt a much quicker response from those you have not heard from. They will either compete for your manuscript or decline. Either way, it will get their attention.

HE WILL EARN EVERY PENNY

How much will an agent charge to represent me?

That is the easiest question of all—the agent gets a straight 15% off the top of your royalties (and your advance if you get one). Relax—they will earn every penny. After selling your book to a publisher (the biggest hurdle), they will track sales and royalties for you. Why? An agent's commission comes from book sales. An agent will act as an accountant in that regard.

If the agent gets paid, it is because your book sells and you get paid. They worry with the numbers and you collect royalty checks. Hopefully, you will be too busy attending book signings and personal speaking engagements to worry about the numbers.

HOW CAN YOU SPOT A BOGUS LITERARY AGENT?

Professional literary agents get paid, but *never* up front. The moment an agent contacts you asking for any kind of fee up front, you may be (most likely are) dealing with a questionable agent. In fact, you are probably dealing with a scam artist. Literary agents make commissions much like real estate agents. If the real estate guy doesn't close the deal and sell a property, he's just burning time and gas. He gets paid when the house sells.

CHECK ENGINE LIGHTS SHOULD START BLINKING

Unlike a real estate agent closing on a house for a homebuyer, when a literary agent sells your book to a publisher, you won't spend a dime—then or ever.

If an agent asks for any kind of fee from an author, *check engine* lights should start blinking. Bogus fees include things like submission reading fees, fees for website design, paid editing service, catalog entry, or book fair showing (agents don't cruise book fairs rummaging through stacks of self-published books looking for the next bestseller). Question the credibility of any literary agent who asks you for any fee, and then run away—fast. That agent is not for real.

There is an exception, according to a recent trend. Some professional agents may include an "up-front expense reimbursement" clause in their contracts, usually $500 or less. Even then, those expenses will be collected only from your advance once a publisher buys your manuscript. They will further stipulate in the contract something along the lines of, "The author will pay no additional expenses without his knowledge or consent." You still pay nothing up front.

ALARMS SHOULD GO OFF IN YOUR HEAD

A true literary agent will gladly provide a verifiable track record of eight to ten sales in the last eighteen months (any less and they are starving). They should be happy to provide a list of published books already sold to traditional publishers. If an agent is reluctant to do so, alarms should go off in your head. Keep in mind, no agent will provide information about an author's manuscript they are in the process of selling to publishers for obvious reasons. It could jeopardize negotiations.

A new agent should be willing to provide information you can verify that he was, for instance, a former editor with a major publisher, or that she worked for a reputable literary agency as a successful agent with a proven record of published books.

The two best online sources I have found about query letters and agents are http://www.agentquery.com and http://www.writerbeware.com. The Agent Query Website has a great list of reputable literary agents who are open to queries and proposals. It is also one of the best places to learn about agents, query letters, book proposals and just about anything to do with writing and publishing books.

The Association of Authors' Representatives, http://www.aaronline.org, is an association most reputable agents belong to. If you don't find a prospective agent's name listed, ask why. Not all agents belong, but most do. It is like a literary agent's Better Business Bureau seal of approval, but non-membership is not a deal breaker.

Michael Hyatt maintains a list of agents who represent Christian authors at http://michaelhyatt.com/literary-agents-who-represent-christian-authors.html. His site is also full of valuable information for authors.

Anywhere else in the world, authors seeking agents should refer to http://www.writersservices.com/agent/

row09/index.htm. As usual, check the references of any prospective agent.

GET READY TO SIT ON THE SLUSH PILE

What if I find a mid-size or small traditional publisher that accepts query letters and proposals from authors?

Get ready to sit on the slush pile of unread book proposals and manuscripts. A slush pile is a sloppy stack of proposals, submissions, and manuscripts an acquisitions editor reaches for when they haven't heard from an agent for a few hours and has a little extra time. That pile does not have an "Urgent, read right away" sign posted nearby. A slush pile is like good cheese; it is aged. Your unpublished book could grow mold on that stack of stuff. Slush piles are on their way out, even though a few small and midsize publishers still accept queries and proposals directly from authors.

WHAT ABOUT WRITING CONTESTS?

Most, if not all, writing contests are designed to take your money. Read the best overview of the pros and cons (mostly cons) of writing contests at http://www.sfwa.org/for-authors/writer-beware/contests/.

I would have a polished non-fiction book proposal ready before I sent out the first batch of query letters. If you get a positive response from an agent, he will want that proposal. For a novel, a completed manuscript is necessary, but in rare cases, an agent may request a fiction book proposal. Be prepared.

CHAPTER 12
DO I NEED A BOOK PROPOSAL?

You don't necessarily need a book proposal if you plan to self-publish, but if you want a shot at being picked up by a traditional publisher, you will need representation by a professional literary agent. If your query letter works and a literary agent takes you on, they will ask you to send a book proposal (especially if you write non-fiction). Why?

Very few traditional publishers will accept proposals or unsolicited manuscripts from authors. They prefer to deal with a literary agent who represents the author. Rejection letters from publishers may refer to you as an "unagented author." The few smaller publishers who are open to new authors will only accept a book proposal (preceded by a query) because acquisition editors don't have time to read entire manuscripts.

As I said in the previous chapter, an agent will only look at your book proposal if a query letter gets his attention. A successful query letter whispers in the agent's ear, *This book will make you lots of money.*

Don't be offended. Writing is a passion—publishing is a business. And please don't say, "I don't want to make money; I just want to help people." If you don't make money on your book, it is because nobody is buying it and that means you aren't helping many people either.

Fiction writers may not need a book proposal. By the way, never say, *I'm writing a fiction novel.* If it's a novel, it is fiction, and vice versa. It is like saying, I'm writing a book book. If an agent responds to a novelist's query letter, a completed manuscript is usually the next thing requested. If you are writing the next great novel, don't send query letters until your manuscript is complete and ready to send.

One reminder: you should invest in a good edit for your manuscript, whether fiction or non-fiction. If your agent sells your manuscript, it will be after the publisher read your proposal and wants to sign you. Then they will want the full manuscript and too many typos could be a turnoff. Some agents will help with the editing, but will really appreciate editing that is already done. Your publisher will do a thorough edit before printing, but the less the editor has to do, the more attractive your manuscript becomes. Remember: it's still about the money.

To recap, non-fiction authors will definitely need a book proposal. If an agent responds to a query letter, they will be more interested in the idea for the book. A completed manuscript is not essential at that time. The agent will only want to see a book proposal, which includes an overview or synopsis of the book. They will tweak your proposal and use it to sell the concept of your non-fiction book to a traditional publisher.

As I said earlier, a good place to find a downloadable

book proposal template is http://michaelhyatt.com/writing-a-winning-book-proposal. Michael Hyatt offers a very popular template for fiction and non-fiction book proposals for only $19.97 each (or both for $29.94). I have used his non-fiction template to create two proposals. As I mentioned, he is a former CEO for Thomas J. Nelson who traditionally publishes about five hundred books each year. He knows what publishers want to see in a proposal.

Alan Rinzlar provides an inside (and somewhat different) view of what publishers want to see in a book proposal at http://www.alanrinzler.com/blog/2008/06/28/the-book-proposal-heres-what-publishers-want/. He has decades of experience as an editor and publisher with major publishing houses.

Mary Embree wrote an article: "The Seven Vital Elements of a Successful Nonfiction Book Proposal." You can read it at http://www.spawn.org/marketing/bookprop.htm.

A little money invested to create a masterful book proposal enhances your chances of becoming a traditionally published author. *Enhances your chances*—I'm a poet and didn't know it. You will read about poets and their poetry in chapter 14. First, let's discuss the place a distributor plays in the publishing process.

CHAPTER 13

DO I NEED A DISTRIBUTOR?

You may need a distributor, but only if you self-publish, and only if your book is selling consistently in certain minimal numbers.

If your book sold close to five hundred copies on Amazon in the first ninety days after publication, and if you are on track to sell two thousand copies the first year, you should try to find a distributor. Any less than two thousand annual sales and you will lose money with a distributor. They require a steep discount in order to persuade bookstores to stock your book. Remember, most bookstores want a 50% discount, so the distributor will want a 65-70% discount to make at least a 15% commission. That still leaves room for profit in your pocket, but only if sales volume is high enough.

BOOKSTORES ONLY DEAL WITH DISTRIBUTORS

There are other things you should know about distributors. Large bookstore chains won't deal with self-publishers or even small independent publishers. They can't be sure the books will meet modern publishing industry standards with a professionally designed cover and expert editing. Neither will they deal with digitally printed books (that eliminates vanity publishers). Plus, they don't, and won't, deal with small orders. Bookstores only deal with distributors.

John Kremer has an extensive list of distributors on his website: http://www.bookmarket.com/distributors.htm.

WHAT IS A BOOK DISTRIBUTOR?

Book distributors are the wholesale link between publishers and the book-buying public. Distributors have catalogs and sales staffs who pitch books directly to bookstore chains. They know what they are doing and have "access" to bookstore buyers.

Access means their sales people present your title nose-to-nose with a buyer from booksellers like Barnes & Noble and Books-A-Million.

BIG DIFFERENCE

There is a mammoth difference between *available* and *access*. Just because a book is available doesn't mean I can buy it off the shelf. "Available" only means your book can be ordered *through* a bookstore. A distributor with "access" can put your book on the shelf at Barnes & Noble. Distributors work hard for their authors and earn a commission from books they sell to bookstore chains.

As a new author, I wouldn't worry too much about getting my book on bookshelves. At best, only 25% of your sales will come from bookstores. Concentrate on the 75%

that will come from online sales, guest appearances on TV and radio, speaking engagements, and your personal efforts to market your book through your own website, social sites like Facebook, and various blogs.

IF YOU DON'T OWN THE ISBN, THE CONVERSATION IS OVER

Did I mention how important it is for you to own the ISBN if you self-publish? *Yes, Ted, about a dozen times.* Well, there is one more reason you should own it. If the day comes when your sales volume justifies finding a distributor, the first question they will ask is, *Do you own the ISBN?* If you don't, the conversation is over. They won't consider carrying your book if anyone else (like a vanity publisher) owns the ISBN. Those books are non-returnable.

You should also be aware that hooking up with a distributor doesn't mean you will have sales. There are no guarantees. They have a rigorous screening process and may not even agree to take you on.

One last word of caution: don't go with an alleged distributor who asks for several hundred dollars to "start the process" or gives some other bogus reason to get into your bank account. True book distributors are also like real estate agents: they don't make a dime until sales generate a profit. Personally, I wouldn't worry too much about joining forces with a distributor unless I get to that wonderful place where my kitchen and dining tables are piled high with books and mailers and I can no longer keep up with sixty orders a day, seven days a week.

CHAPTER 14

POETRY IS FOR
(POOR) POETS

Writing and publishing poetry is a challenge all its own.
Only certain publishers will consider poetry because
books of rhyme are not big sellers in publishing. Poets are
passionate about their work and are among the first to be
inspired by the great masters of rhyme. True to Robert
Frost, if you decide to write and publish your poetry, you
will have seen two roads diverging in the literary woods
and will have taken the one less followed.

POETS DON'T MAKE MUCH MONEY ON
THEIR POETRY

I try not to be negative, but poets don't make much money
on their poetry. That raises the question: *do you want to
write poetry or do you want to make money?* Sadly, the less-
traveled road of poetry-penning leads through financially
lean (less green) pastures.

At the same time, life has taught us one simple rule:
money isn't everything, but you need money to put butter
on your toast. Yet, current history tells the ominous stories
of several of the richest and most famous among us who
took their own lives because something was missing,

something prosperity and fame couldn't buy.

Poets write for the sheer love of making lyrics sing directly to the heart. So, if you are one of those giving people who loves to write poetry, chances are you have found a great secret—the joy of doing what you love. Keep your day job for sure, but keep writing for certain.

The *Empty Mirror Arts Magazine & Books* paints an optimistic picture of the possibilities for poets as well as some good advice on how to publish poetry at http://www.emptymirrorbooks.com/publishing/advice.html. The site also offers more information on how to write poetry and how to get feedback on your poems at http://www.emptymirrorbooks.com/publishing/writing-poetry.html.

Dr. Louie Crew, emeritus professor at Rutgers University, lists over eight hundred poetry publishers who accept electronic submissions at http://andromeda.rutgers.edu/~lcrew/pbonline.html. His website also offers extensive information and advice for poets.

Another useful website is http://www.poets.org/.

WHAT ABOUT E-BOOKS?

The growing popularity of downloadable books has leveled the playing field for poets. In 2012, 25% of books purchased were downloaded by people with Kindles or Nooks or any of a number of e-book readers. You can convert your poetry to an online e-book for around $100. My guess is, people who love to read poetry will download a $3 or $4 poetry e-book without a moment's hesitation. Go for it. I might even try some rhyme myself. Here goes.

I wrote a book, but it didn't cook. I hoped it would sell, but it's too soon to tell. It was a real honey, but it didn't make any money. I thought I could write, but no one saw the light. Alas, I must embrace my potential fate: Did I start too late to be a literary great? Reality is biting, but I will not stop writing. I started e-booking, and folks started looking. What a stroke of luck; I just made a buck.

Getting your poems published is difficult because so few publishers will take a chance on poetry. Give e-books a chance to showcase your talent for rhyme.

Poetry is a challenge because of publishers' reluctance to publish; writing children's books is a challenge for a different reason.

CHAPTER 15
CHILDREN'S BOOKS ARE UNIQUE

It surprises me how many people are passionate about writing and publishing children's picture books. I'm not talking about smaller-sized books a parent would read to a child. Larger sizes like 8x10, 10x8, or 8x8 are the norm for picture books. They are shorter as well. Average word count for picture books for one to six-year-olds is 400–500. For first through fifth graders, the range is 800–2000 words. Even with the low word count of children's books, there are unique challenges that authors face.

COST TO PRINT IS HIGHER

Because color illustrations (10–12 per book) are a necessary part of a children's picture book, the cost to print is higher. The only way to market your children's book online is through a distributor, and that will require minimum sales of two thousand books per year.

The necessity for a distributor has to do with the digital print cost per book. It is generally too high to make online print on demand sales profitable. Amazon, for instance, requires a 55% discount to offer a book online. If your book cost $6 to print digitally and you charged

$10 retail, Amazon would want it for $4.50 ($1.50 less than your print cost). Barnes & Noble will want to buy at a 50% discount, or $5. The numbers don't work for you.

Check out children's book pricing at your local bookstore. You will find few, if any, over $9.99 (most will be in the $5–$8 range), so you can see the challenge, whether you sell it in bookstores or online.

The only way to offer it online and not lose money is to print enough to reach a low enough print cost per book that a distributor might consider taking you on.

You could spend several thousand dollars just to get a few hundred books printed when you include what a professional illustrator would charge. You need good illustrations to compete visually with the other children's books already on the shelf.

There are ways to cut costs. You could visit your local college or university if they offer graphic art or digital media courses, and pay a student to do your illustrations. You might be surprised at the available talent right under your nose. Students would get extra credit for outside work and save you money in the process.

TRADITIONAL PUBLISHERS PRINT THOUSANDS AT A TIME

How can color-illustrated children's books sell at such low prices in bookstores? Traditional publishers print thousands at a time and that keeps print costs down. The average person can't afford printing 10,000 to 20,000 copies.

Your best choice is printing what you can afford and doing your own marketing. Ron Pramschufer at selfpublishing.com suggests you need a marketing plan to sell between five and ten thousand copies of your children's book.

Nick Katsoris, a very successful children's book author, tells you how to market your book in his article, "7 Steps to Children's Book Success" at http://www.selfgrowthengine.com/professional-growth/self-publishing/articles/7-steps-childrens-book-success.

If your children's book takes off, securing a distributor is the only practical way to go. Selling just five thousand books on your own will be a full-time job. Not impossible, but you would need to work hard and build sales gradually. Don't plan on getting a lot of sleep.

As you can see, there are challenges for children's book authors, most of them financial. Yet, with persistence you can be a successful children's book author.

The *Children's Books* page at the selfpublishing.com website is also a great source of information, including print pricing for different sizes and specifications: **www.selfpublishing.com/childrens/printing/**. Digital printing has made children's books a more economical possibility and Ron Pramschufer believes the day will come when it is a financially viable goal for self-published authors.

You might consider joining **SCBWI.org,** the Society of Children's Book Writers and Illustrators. Cost is $85 annually. You can learn from SCBWI, even as a non-member.

Children's books are not yet practical as e-books, in my opinion. They are available as e-books and will fit the small e-readers, but I doubt kids will really appreciate a tiny Kermit the Frog or a miniature Little Red Riding Hood strolling through the woods. The iPad, with its ten-inch screen is more practical and is a better platform for children's books.

Even so, the jury is still out in 2015 whether many folks will buy children's books for e-readers. Most parents I have talked to, including those who are avid Kindlers and Nookers, still want their children to see and touch the beautiful multi-colored illustrations as they turn each page to get an eyeful of the next visual treat. This suggests many parents believe paper children's books provide an intimacy that electronic devices don't.

That said, e-books are here to stay, so let's talk about the great new opportunity for first-time authors to put their books in electronic print at a very reasonable cost, because no paper or ink is required (remember, paper is half the cost of printing a book).

CHAPTER 16
E-BOOKS ARE HERE TO STAY

I visited a local Florida church recently on a bright Sunday morning. I hadn't been there in years. A smiling face greeted me with, "Ted Bowman!" He knew me and while he looked familiar, I was at a loss. When he told me his name, I realized I hadn't seen him in almost fifty years. We had been college classmates back in the sixties.

After a brief trip down memory lane, I gave him my card and said, "Email me."

He replied, without apology, "I don't do that computer stuff."

I wasn't offended or surprised. He will probably never be a Kindle customer.

I worked for a small South Carolina lumber company for a short time back in the 1990s. The owner was old, old school. He still used a black telephone with a rotary dial, a hand-crank adding machine, and he refused to even consider a computer to modernize his business. He wrote out monthly billing statements by hand on carbon copy invoices. It was a nostalgic trip back in time. To his credit, he never had a computer crash.

When this wonderful gentleman retired, his son

quickly ordered a touchtone phone, a computer to track sales and print out monthly statements, and an electronic register for daily cash transactions. That stately old lumber company reluctantly ventured into the twenty-first century. His father didn't like it, but customers cheered. You can't stop progress. Sooner or later, that train will come down the track.

WHAT DO THESE STORIES HAVE TO WITH E-BOOKS?

The e-book train is on track and moving right along. These newfangled electronic books didn't catch on as quickly as some had predicted, but once on the market, e-books and e-readers have grown in popularity and have leveled off after capturing 25% of the total book market.

PAPERBACKS ARE STILL ALIVE AND WELL

Bookstores are closing at a steady rate, not so much because of e-books, but because most readers are buying e-books *and* paperbacks online. Bottom line: people are reading books of every kind, currently, three "dead tree" books for every e-book.

If you have published a paperback book, check into converting it to an e-book. I converted my last book and will convert this book as soon as it's published. Do you realize you can publish an e-book for about $200 and offer it online at Amazon, Barnes & Noble, Sony, iBook (for Mac), and several other online stores? If it sells, you can always do a print version. All you need is a well-designed cover and your edited manuscript in Microsoft

Word. A PDF file will work, but will cost a little extra to convert.

THE INK VERSUS PIXEL WAR

There are those who predict e-books will eventually be the death of paper books. They said moving pictures would be the end of live stage performances, but Broadway's theater district lights are brighter than ever. They said television would make radios a thing of the past. Do you own one of those new-fangled horseless carriages? Chances are, if it has wheels and an engine, it has a radio. So does every home, office, combine, boat and space shuttle (not really sure about the space shuttle).

THEIR HEADS BOB MINDLESSLY

I will admit, cassettes replaced eight-tracks and now cds have replaced cassettes, and IPods have replaced the old Walkman but that doesn't mean no one listens to music anymore. Many adults and most teenagers can't seem to function without little plugs in their ears that make their heads bob mindlessly to a mysterious, undetectable tempo.

Music is here to stay and so is the written word. It just depends on how you listen to songs and how you choose to read words. Either way, song writers and authors will be in demand for the foreseeable future and so will songs and books, in one form or another. Now we are ready to consider the big question and the whole reason I wrote this chapter.

Do I need an e-book version of my just published book?

Yes, you do.

Is it difficult?

Not for people who know how to do the techy stuff. It's like vinyl flooring. I know how to build stud walls, build and install custom cabinets, lay brick and block, finish concrete, ply shingles, hang and finish sheetrock and just about everything else involved in building a house from the ground up.

There are some things I won't attempt, and installing vinyl flooring is one of them. I tried it a time or two, but it was very difficult and not worth the nerve-wracking time and effort it took to figure out how to do it right.

I look at e-books the same way. When it comes to e-book conversion, I hire an expert.

John Kremer lists e-book conversion companies at http://www.bookmarket.com/e-books.htm.

Does my e-book need an ISBN?

You will need a new ISBN for your e-book (and, yes, you still need to own that ISBN). Even though it is an electronic reproduction of your paper book, it is in a different format, thus the need for a new ISBN. It is the same as needing one ISBN for your paperback version and another for the hardback, even though it is the same book.

Don't you wish you had gone ahead and bought a block of ten ISBNs to start with?

Certain questions still hang in the air about e-book ISBNs. Some insist you need a different ISBN for each e-book format. If that is the case, an author would need to provide two different numbers, one for the EPUB format and one for the ePDF format. Amazon uses a tweaked EPUB file called Mobi, but they don't require an ISBN. The ePDF format is used almost exclusively by educational entities (schools) and is not necessary unless your book would be useful in education as a downloadable book for students. An ePDF file is still necessary for older, pre-2008, e-readers. That lowers the number of necessary ISBNs to only two.

Liz Bury, a British journalist, wrote an article in March 2010 about the future of ISBNs and e-books titled "'E-book ISBN Mess Still Needs Sorting Out,' say UK publishers" at http://publishingperspectives. com/2010/03/e-book-isbn-mess-needs-sorting-out-say-uk-publishers/. The article suggests most booksellers and wholesalers would like an ISBN for each format, but publishers prefer using only one. So far, the publishers are winning the debate.

Ron Pramschufer, of selfpublishing.com, leans toward the eventual probability that e-books might need multiple ISBNs, but thinks one will do for now. I agree.

AMAZON MAKES THE ISBN OPTIONAL

As I mentioned, schools and older e-readers (pre 2008) use the ePDF format. Amazon makes the ISBN optional and uses their own internal tracking number called an ASIN (Amazon Standard Identification Number). It is a ten-figure combination of letters and numbers. With Amazon, the ISBN is a token number with no purpose. Save your money and plan on one ISBN for now.

Bookbaby.com did my last e-book conversion and they only required one ISBN for the numerous e-book sellers who now offer my book, including Amazon's Kindle. The whole process is simple. I supplied a high resolution cover image 800-1000 pixels tall and 550-700 pixels wide (their minimal specifications). I uploaded my edited manuscript in Word, and one ISBN. The experts did the rest. The whole process took two to four weeks and only cost me $99. As of January, 2015, Bookbaby charges $249 for conversion and takes no commission from online sales.

AUTHORS RECEIVE E-BOOK ROYALTIES EVERY TWO WEEKS

There is an extra charge ($50 to $100) if you upload a PDF file of your content. You decide the retail price (I stay below five dollars). Authors receive royalties every two weeks (deposited directly into your bank account or PayPal). Average royalties are $2-$3 per sale on a $5 e-book.

Don't forget, you can produce an e-book even if you don't publish a paperback first. As I said, you will need a high-resolution cover and an edited manuscript in Word (e-book converters will create your cover for around $150).

Don't be tempted to bypass editing just to save money. E-book readers will notice typos and never buy another book from you.

There are writers making a good living just selling e-books. They are popular because readers can download a book and start reading in mere minutes. No waiting for the mailman and no shipping charges.

Whether you write an e-book or a paper book, you will need a marketing plan. Just because you wrote it, doesn't necessarily mean anyone outside your immediate circle of friends and family will buy it.

CHAPTER 17

IF YOU WRITE IT,
THEY ~~WILL~~ *MIGHT*
COME

When it comes to book marketing: if you don't do it, it doesn't get done. Remember, vanity publishers lead you to believe your book will be on the shelf at Barnes & Noble. You already know it won't. It will be available if someone orders it. If people don't know about your book, they won't order it. Honest publishers will tell you marketing is your responsibility, not theirs.

I have a friend who paid a vanity publisher an extra $1500 for marketing and did not understand why he couldn't find his book on the shelf at Barnes & Noble. After all, he paid extra for "distribution," to make his book "available to 25,000 bookstores nationwide." His sales were weak. We have already discussed that slick, double-talk sales ploy. Your book will be available to thousands of bookstores in a database only, but not on any shelf anywhere.

A GROWING TREND

There is a growing trend worth mentioning. Traditional publishers are starting to notice self-published books that have good sales. More and more self-published authors are being offered publishing contracts. M.J. Rose, founder and president of AuthorBuzz.com, wrote an article in 2002 about the growing phenomenon of major publishers contacting self-published authors whose books were selling well. By now, the trend is even more prominent.

I found two websites where new authors can list their books in hopes of being picked up by traditional publishers who allegedly scan these lists looking for new books with potential. The sites are http://www.writersEdgeService.com and http://www.ChristianManuscriptSubmissions.com. The cost to be listed with either company is $95-$98 every six months. Some writers have been picked up by publishers from these lists. You are required to submit a book proposal (not a full manuscript).

It could work for you. Make sure your proposal is well-written and professionally edited. Even if you don't submit to one of these websites, writing a proposal will give you a more professional mindset as an author.

I can't explain it, but creating a book proposal changed my whole attitude toward writing.

Both websites require agents and publishers to fill out a thorough screening form before they can enter to view book proposals, so the likelihood of questionable agents or shady publishers getting in is remote. However, it never hurts to be vigilant.

If a publisher or someone claiming to be a literary agent contacts you claiming to have seen your book proposal on one of these sites and asks for money up front to publish your book, or to represent you, they are a vanity publisher or a less-than-honest agent and should be avoided. If that happens, let the website monitor know. In my opinion, you are better off following the query letter process. It's free.

In the past, professional literary agents (almost) never contacted authors initially. On rare occasions, an agent may hear about a promising manuscript and contact the author. In my original manuscript for this book, I said, "I estimate it happens about as often as a solar eclipse." When my editor read my "solar eclipse" remark she left this footnote: "Ted, this is no longer true. I can think of at least four times right off the top of my head, and know plenty of agents who do this." The tide is shifting in favor of authors. Self-publishing can be a door-opener to a traditional contract.

No matter which direction you take, buy *1001 Ways to Market Your Book* by John Kremer, and plan on doing your own marketing. I also encourage you to subscribe to John's monthly marketing tips newsletter at http://www.bookmarket.com. His advice is gold.

Another good book on this aftermarket is Brian Jud's updated version of *Beyond The Bookstore* titled, *How to Make Real Money Selling Books (Without Worrying About Returns)*. It is the ultimate do-it-yourself guide to selling your books to non-bookstore buyers in large quantities with no returns. Not just who to contact, but when and how. Learn more at http://www.bookmarketingworks.com/HTMRMSB.htm.

If you have financial resources to promote your

book, check out Fern Reiss's Web site at http://www.publishinggame.com. She is a master publicist. Her website offers several great books, as well as free articles and resources for authors.

Here is some trivia for you newbies. A Commodore 64 computer was an eight-bit home computer introduced in 1982. During the mid-1980s, I sold software programs to businesses for a couple of Basic language programmers. The fastest computers at the time were the IBM PC and the IBM compatible Tandy 1000 made by Radio Shack. Each had a blazing four megahertz-per-second processing speed and used a 5.25" floppy disk (earlier disks were eight inches; earliest disks were 12"). Neither had a hard drive. An additional hard drive with ten to twenty megabytes capacity was a factory option. The programmers I worked for bought an eight megabyte external hard drive and were amazed at the capacity. That's eight megabytes, not eight gigabytes.

In case you are wondering where the term "floppy" came from, these discs were made of paper-thin flexible plastic and they actually flopped back and forth if you shook them. Radio Shack later came out with the Tandy 2000 model with an unbelievable computing speed of eight megahertz per second. One of the programmers I worked for in the early 1980s asked, "How fast are these things going to get?"

That same programmer, a trained technician in mainframe maintenance, installed one of the first commercial computers at our local hospital. It had an eighty megabyte hard drive that easily handled all hospital records and business. Today you can't even buy a thumb drive less than one gig. Like I said, things are changing.

I mentioned the above trivia to show how far we have come in technology and to give your brain a rest from publishing. Enough rest. Let's talk about websites and whether you, as an author, should have one. Today, the average person can have his own website for pennies a day.

CHAPTER 18

DO I NEED A WEBSITE?

Yes, you do. Having your own website puts you on a level playing field with every other business on the Internet and potentially exposes your book to millions of readers. You can buy a domain name with your book title and direct traffic to your site where you will make the most money from each book sale. If local bookstores carry your book, you should also list them with their phone numbers.

You can purchase a domain name from http://www.godaddy.com (recommended) for $10-$15 per year. (Go Daddy also offers economical websites with hosting as does Wordpress) If the domain name you seek is already taken, you can change your title slightly and keep entering names until you get the one that includes your title.

A FOUR OR FIVE PAGE WEBSITE WILL DO

Remember, you don't need a massive website to sell one book. A four or five page website will do. Make sure it has a page for book purchases (shopping cart). PayPal will help you set up to take credit cards at no charge. I have used them for years with no problems. Use one page to showcase book details and why you wrote it. A *Contact* page and an *About* page should be part of your site, all undergirded by a simple, informative *Home page*.

For those on a tight budget, selfpublishing.com now offers a completely free website to market your book with free hosting (if you publish with them). They are among the few self-publishing companies I recommend. Art Bookbindery does the same thing. Warren Drake of Vision Resources Network (http://www.visionresources. net) offers several economical options. He will build and maintain a website for you, or he will train you to build and maintain your own site. I went with the latter option and have complete control of my website.

BUY YOUR OWN DOMAIN NAME

If you pay someone to design your site, it is still imperative that you buy your own domain name. Do not let a designer supply a domain name, even if it's free. Why? If someone else owns the domain name, you may not be able to use it if you want a new website. Stuff happens. You could have a falling out with your current web designer, and they may charge you an arm and a leg just to transfer the domain name to you. If they chose to, they could refuse to transfer at all. You would have to start over with a new website and new domain name.

You want your website to attract and keep visitors so they will buy your products, or services you are offering. Don't leave the total makeup of your website to your web designer. Website developers are often more concerned with how it looks than how it works.

New technology has given rookie website designers, fresh out of school, all kinds of bells and whistles to incorporate into websites (much of which surfers I have talked to don't like). More often than not, these designers are concerned about what looks cool, and are oblivious to what works well and makes a simple, user-friendly website. The average designer also has little or no training in what we call SEO (Search Engine Optimization). Search engines like Google, Yahoo, or Microsoft's Bing help surfers find websites. You type in the information you are looking for and a search engine tries to send you in the right direction. Search Engine Optimization helps you get the most out of your search. Websites with improper keyword hints, unrelated meta-tags, and poorly worded page titles, make finding that website difficult.

Simple Web design rules to follow:

1. *It should be easy on the eyes.* Use dark fonts and light backgrounds. Black print on a white background works best. Remember, people come to a website to get information or buy something. A nice color scheme is important, but should make visitors comfortable, not put them into a psychedelic trance. Don't use fonts that are very small or very large and don't use all caps. Visitors will think you are yelling.

   Reading website pages with white (or light) print against a black (or dark) background slows readers down and takes longer to read. I personally run from sites like that. If you use light print on dark backgrounds, do so very sparingly. It's a nice contrast as long as you don't overdo it. Too much can make your eyes bleed. Not really, but you get my point.

2. *It should be easy to navigate.* Put a menu on every page and also a separate home page link at the bottom. Don't use a splash page that simply "welcomes" visitors to the site, along with an "Enter Site" link. No one wants to wait for a page to load, then have to click again to get to your home page.

   While you are at it, don't have jumping frogs, blinking lights, or flaming fonts. Okay, sometimes hip-hopping frogs, flashing lights, or blazing words might be useful to get a reader's attention, but I would use them very, very sparingly. They tend to irritate visitors, as do pop-ups. After dealing with the second pop-up ad, I leave and so do many visitors, I suspect.

3. *Don't force your visitors to listen to music or video.* Music or video I can't turn off drives me up a wall. Streaming video is fine if it is necessary for informational instruction or live sessions visitors came intentionally to view. Keep it simple and quiet! Some Web designers think things like flash pages, moving images, and cute sounds are groovy. Most web surfers don't.

4. *Tell your visitors quickly and simply what your site is about.* You have only a few seconds to get their attention. Surfers are skimmers and won't read every word. They look for bullet points or highlights. They know what they are looking for, so give them what they want. If they can't find what they are looking for quickly and easily, they won't stay. Again, you have only a few seconds to get their attention. Give them a clean, simple home page that explains what your site is about and clear links and directions to find related information.

   Put your contact information at the top or bottom of every page. A visitor may want to call or email you on impulse if a particular page clicks with them. Look at the bottom of any page on my website, http://www. jcpublishers.net. You will find my contact info, including a clickable email link (don't show your actual email).

5. *Avoid the use of Flash pages.* Why? Several reasons, not the least of which is the fact that all-Flash websites will be ignored by most search engines. To be fair, Google has found a way to read text in Flash, but most other search engines haven't. Your wonderful, cutting-edge, all-Flash website will be virtually invisible to millions of surfers.

Flash sites are also inaccessible from many mobile phones and devices. Cutting-edge website developers love Flash—*surfers don't.* I won't stay on a website that forces me to chase menu items with my mouse, or pesters my peripheral vision with moving graphics or pictures.

Just for fun, see what you do not want your website to look like at http://www.websitesthatsuck.com. I am amazed at some of the expensive websites that made that list. Just remember one thing: keep it simple. You just want people to buy your book.

CHAPTER 19
COULD YOU REPEAT THAT?

I'm one of those people who likes to see everything condensed and made simple. It occurred to me, you might like to see this whole book condensed into one chapter so here goes:

1. FIRST THINGS FIRST. Go to your local bookstore and make sure your book is different and better than anything else on the shelf. Go ahead and write a book proposal (I know you've been thinking about it).

2. DECISION TIME. Decide, right now, whether to self-publish or go for a contract with one of the big boys. If you go the traditional route and land a contract, you won't need to self-publish your book. If you self-publish first, you can still go for the gold later.

3. THE MONEY FUNNELS THROUGH THE ISBN. Buy your own ISBN. If you don't, I'm glad you already paid for this book, because after one of those X&@ ZJ%+# vanity outfits fleeces you to publish a so-so book, you will be too broke to buy a pencil.

4. EDITING IS A MUST. Edit it or don't publish it. Use a real book editor while you're at it.

5. YOU *CAN* JUDGE A BOOK BY ITS COVER. Pay for a good cover design. That way, potential buyers

will open your book, even if it's not that good. If it isn't that good, tweak it until it is, then publish it with that exquisite cover.

6. THE BIG FIB. Don't believe anything a vanity publisher tells you. I'll be nice and say that they are confused about the truth. Sales experts at seminars will tell you, *all buyers are liars*. I never heard a seminar speaker say, *so are sellers*. Enter, vanity publishers.

I used to sell cars with a buddy who told prospective buyers, "The engine block in this car is the same block they put in Indy 500 race cars" (It was a straight six-cylinder.) I still laugh when I think about his claim. Some actually believed it.

7. NEEDLE IN A HAYSTACK. You *can* find a needle in a haystack, that true self-publisher. Ask the deal-breaking question: *Can I use my own ISBN?* True self-publishing companies (facilitators) will always say *yes* without hesitation. Vanity reps will dance around the question and, when cornered, will always say no.

8. ALL PRINTERS ARE NOT CREATED EQUAL. There is more than one way to skin a cat or print a book. You can print with a digital printer (uses toner and heat) or offset printer (uses ink and no heat). Short print runs (499 books or less) will be digitally printed. Larger print runs (five hundred books and up) should be printed offset. Keep in mind, you don't need that many books to start with. One or two hundred will work just fine and they will be digitally printed. No big deal. If your book takes off, you can always print offset when demand requires it.

9. LIGHTNING SOURCE STRIKES. Lightning Source prints most digital books for the majority of publishers. With your own ISBN, you can become a Lightning Source publisher and use their print service, but you

don't have to. You can always hook up with them later if your book takes off and you need lots of inexpensive copies for your personal sales. If you publish traditionally, your publisher will supply copies.

10. HOW BIG SHOULD MY BOOK BE? Your book should not be too big. A 150 to 200 page book is what the average reader prefers. When you become a famous, best-selling author, you can write all the big tomes you want. For now, short and sweet is the name of the writing game for new authors.

11. DO I NEED A LITERARY AGENT? You need a literary agent to help you go for the gold, that nice contract with a traditional publisher. You can break into that exclusive, elusive club if you are patient and tenacious, and have rhino skin at least one inch thick.

12. DO I NEED A BOOK PROPOSAL? You need a book proposal if you seek representation by a literary agent. No proposal, no agent. If I don't say it you will be disappointed: *go ahead and write a proposal, even if you self-publish.* You can thank me later.

13. DO I NEED A DISTRIBUTOR? You might need a distributor, but only if you are selling a ton of books (at least 165 a month for a year). Any less than that and you will lose money.

14. POETRY IS FOR (POOR) POETS: Poets don't get rich writing poetry. 'Nuf said, but where would we be without poetry? Go for it, you purveyors of rhyme.

15. CHILDREN'S BOOKS ARE UNIQUE. Children's books are a challenge, mostly because of the extra cost to print color illustrations, and because the average children's book sells for around $5. A children's book writer will pay $6-$10 to print the few copies they can afford. Commercial publishers print thousands at a time

and do so for less than a dollar each. That is why they still make money at $5 retail. You can still be successful though.

16. E-BOOKS ARE HERE TO STAY. Deal with it. Turn your "dead tree" book into bits and bytes and make some money off your worded Picasso. It's cheap to produce an e-book.

17. IF YOU WRITE IT, THEY ~~WILL~~ *MIGHT* COME. Just because you wrote it doesn't mean folks will run out and buy it. You must become a marketing expert by listening to marketing experts and doing what they recommend. Sell, sell, and sell some more.

    I worked in insurance as a salesman and a sales manager. When I became a manager (working more hours for less pay—*what was I thinking?*), I had one agent who sold so much insurance, I thought he was cheating. I found out the first day I worked with him, he asked everybody he met, all day long, to buy insurance and a bunch of them did. If you are uncomfortable asking people to buy your book, get over it and start asking.

18. DO I NEED A WEBSITE? Yes, you do. Find a way to get one. Before proceeding with website building, buy your own domain name (right after you buy your own ISBN).

19. *Could you summarize your book, Ted?* I just did.

Now, get to work and finish that manuscript. Don't make me come over there and get in your face.

CHAPTER 20
JUST DO IT

Only you can convince yourself your book is worth writing. Chances are, you have stopped midway through your manuscript because you lost interest, got bored, had a brain-freeze, or just gave up. You stopped being the little engine that could. Who told you it would be easy? If you get bored, take a break for a week or a month or more. It will look and feel fresh when you get back to it.

There is one other possibility. You haven't even started, haven't written a word. You know what you want to write about. You know someone else has written about the subject, but you are convinced you can do a better job. So what are you waiting for? Every author fights *inertia:* indisposition to motion, exertion, or change.

Sitting around talking about how much you want to write a book reminds me of a hound dog sitting on a thorn. It bothers him, but he is too lazy to get off his rump and ease the pain, so he just sits there howling. Overcome your inertia: get off your rump, start writing and change your stars forever.

WRITE SOMETHING TODAY

This is for the multitudes of would-be authors who say, "I need to get started on my book, the one I decided to write

__ years ago" (you fill in the number). Write something today. Go to your computer. Turn it on. Pull up whatever Word version you have (I still use Word 2010). Now, take a deep breath. You are about to change your life.

1. Write an introduction to your book within the next ten minutes. What do you want your book to say? That is your introduction. Stop what you are doing (unless you are a surgeon in the middle of a heart transplant) and *write the first line of your introduction.*

TED, I HAVE TO THINK ABOUT IT.

Stop making excuses; you've thought about it long enough.

What? You say you don't have a computer? Get out a blank piece of paper and write something—anything to do with what your book is about. If you want to write about fish, start with, "I do know fish. I know how to catch 'em, clean 'em, cook 'em, eat 'em, and things of that nature. I do know fish."

2. Now, pick a title for the first chapter and write the first sentence of chapter one. Don't worry about how stupid it sounds.

   Example: FISH ARE COOL. Water is a good cooling agent.

3. Pick a title for chapter two and write the first sentence. FISH ARE WET. Water keeps them hydrated.

4. Next, stop writing (if you can), pick up the phone and tell someone, "I finally started writing my book today! I'm already working on the second chapter. It's all about fish."

5. Lastly, lean back and take pride in your accomplishment. Pat yourself on the back; you just got off your thorn.

Most people who say they want to write a book never get that far.

Are you one of them? Not if you did what I asked and wrote that introduction and the first two chapter titles. You are on your way to publishing your first book. Now, think of a title for chapter three and write the first sentence.

How about: FISH ARE TASTY. I like to eat 'em.

Don't worry about grammar, punctuation, or spelling. The more you worry about grammar, the less inspired you will be. Just write. Rik Feeney, speaking to our local writers group, suggested you turn off your spell-checker and grammar function. Get rid of anything that distracts you. If that doesn't work, he dares you to turn off your monitor and write blind. Your deepest thoughts are more important than your grammar skills at this stage. Leave a little work for your editor.

Still having trouble writing? Grit your teeth and pump out that book proposal. The planks to your manuscript will fall neatly into place after that. Before you know it, your first book will arrive. It won't be too long before you start thinking how much better your next book will be. Just do it!

RESOURCE LINKS FOR SELF-PUBLISHERS

GREAT MONTHLY NEWSLETTERS

John Kremer: http://www.bookmarket.com
Patricia Fry: http://www.spawn.org/

ISBN OWNERSHIP BY COUNTRY OF RESIDENCE

USA: www.bowker.com
GREAT BRITAIN: http://www.isbn.nielsenbook.co.uk/
controller.php?page=123
New Zealand:
http://www.natlib.govt.nz/services/get-advice/
publishers
Australia: http://www.thorpe.com.au
Worldwide: http://isbn-information.com/isbn-agency.
html

EDITING

Donna Goodrich: http://www.thewritersfriend.net/
Anna Genoese: http://www.annagenoese.com/
David Sluka: http://www.hitthemarkpublishing.com
http://www.selfpublishing.com/editorial/

GHOST WRITERS

David Sluka: http://www.hitthemarkpublishing.com
Misty Powell: mysti5d@gmail.com

GRAMMAR HELP

Chicago Manual of Style Online ($35 annually): http://
www.chicagomanualofstyle.org/home.html
The Purdue Online Writing Lab: http://owl.english.
purdue.edu/owl/resource/551/01

PROPER ABBREVIATIONS OF THE BOOKS OF THE BIBLE

http://hbl.gcc.edu/abbreviationsCHICAGO.htm
http://www.aresearchguide.com/bibleabb.html

WRITING TIPS AND HELP

Audrey Owen: http://www.writershelper.com/
writingtips.html
Donna Goodrich: http://www.thewritersfriend.net/
Terry Whalin: http://www.right-writing.com/
Michael Hyatt's advice to first-time authors: http://
michaelhyatt.com/advice-to-first-time-authors.html

TRUE SELF-PUBLISHING FACILITATORS

http://www.selfpublishing.com
http://www.artbookbindery.com
http://www.BethanyPress.com
http://www.bookmasters.com
http://www.morrispublishing.com

BOOK PROMOTION SERVICES

Fern Reiss: http://www.publishinggame.com/promote.htm

Her website, books, and articles are great resources for authors.

GO FOR THE GOLD RESOURCE LINKS

BOOK PROPOSAL HELP

Michael Hyatt: www.michaelhyatt.com
William Cane: http://www.hiwrite.com/index.html
Terry Whalin: http://www.bookproposals.ws/
Patricia Fry: http://www.spawn.org

WEBSITES AUTHORS CAN SUBMIT PROPOSALS TO

http://writersedgeservice.com/publist.htm
http://www.christianmanuscriptsubmissions.com

QUERY LETTERS

Charlotte Dillon: http://www.charlottedillon.com/query.html

Lynn Flewelling: http://www.sfwa.org/2005/01/the-complete-nobodys-guide-to-query-letters/

How to write a query letter: http://www.agentquery.com/writer_hq.aspx

What to do if an agent calls: http://www.agentquery.com/writer_or.aspx

LITERARY AGENT LISTS

Full agent search at Agent Query: http://www.agentquery.com/search_advanced.aspx

Agents who represent Christian authors: http://michaelhyatt.com/literary-agents-who-represent-christian-authors.html

World-wide agent list: http://www.writersservices.com/agent/row09/index.htm

ADVICE FROM FOUR PROFESSIONAL LITERARY AGENTS:

http://terrywhalin.blogspot.com/

http://chipmacgregor.typepad.com/

http://www.rachellegardner.com/

http://michaelhyatt.com/before-you-hire-a-literary-agent.html

INDEPENDENT BOOK DISTRIBUTORS LIST

John Kremer: http://www.bookmarket.com/distributors.htm

POETS AND POETRY

Good advice on how to publish your poetry:
http://www.emptymirrorbooks.com/publishing/advice.html.

Information on How to write poetry well and How to get feedback on your poems:
http://www.emptymirrorbooks.com/publishing/writing-poetry.html.

Dr. Louie Crew, emeritus professor at Rutgers University,

lists over 800 poetry publishers who accept electronic submissions: http://andromeda.rutgers.edu/~lcrew/pbonline.html

One more useful website: http://www.poets.org/.

CHILDREN'S BOOKS

Nick Katsoris's article, "7 Steps to Children's Book Success": http://www.selfgrowthengine.com/professional-growth/self-publishing/articles/7-steps-childrens-book-success.

Print pricing for different sizes and specifications: www.selfpublishing.com/childrens/printing/.

TIPS FOR WRITING CHILDREN'S PICTURE BOOKS

http://www.memfox.com/so-you-want-to-write-a-picture-book.html

http://www.patmora.com/tips/

http://www.writing-world.com/children/backes1.shtml

CHILDREN'S BOOK ILLUSTRATORS

http://www.selfpublishing.com/childrens/illustration/illustrators.php

Valerie Bouthyette: http://www.vbouthyette.com or vbouthyette@stny.rr.com

Justin Currie: Justin_currie@hotmail.com or 866-944-2999

You might consider joining SCBWI, Society of Children's Book Writers and Illustrators: http://www.scbwi.org

CHILDREN'S BOOK AGENTS LIST

http://aseraserburns.wordpress.com/2010/09/13/top-20-picture-book-agents-in-publishers-marketplace/

E-BOOKS AND THE ISBN QUESTION

Liz Bury article, "'E-book ISBN Mess Still Needs Sorting Out,' say UK publishers": http://publishingperspectives.com/2010/03/e-book-isbn-mess-needs-sorting-out-say-uk-publishers/

E-BOOK CONVERSION

John Kremer's extensive list (not necessarily endorsed by him): http://www.bookmarket.com/e-books.htm

DYNAMITE MARKETING RESOURCES

John Kremer, 1001 Ways To Market Your Book, available on his website: http://www.bookmarket.com.
Fern Reiss: http://publishinggame.com/promote.htm
Brian Jud, Beyond The Bookstore (updated version How to Make Real Money Selling Books (Without Worrying About Returns), available on his website: http://www.bookmarketingworks.com/HTMRMSB.htm

OWN YOUR OWN WEBSITE

http://www.selfpublishing.com
http://www.visionresources.net
http://www.godaddy.com

COMMON SENSE WEBSITE DESIGN RULES

http://www.websitesthatsuck.com

COPYRIGHT

http://www.copyright.gov/ (DIY for $35 as of 2012)

LIBRARY OF CONGRESS CATALOGUE NUMBER

http://www.loc.gov/publish/
(Good to have; don't need unless you plan to sell your book to 16,000 public libraries)

CITATIONS PAGE

[1]Michael Hyatt, original complimentary book proposal template offered by Thomas Nelson Publishers in 1998 titled "The Write Stuff," page 7.

[2]Public domain.

[3]http://michaelhyatt.com/four-strategies-for-creating-titles-that-jump-off-the-page.html.

[4]"© 2013, Michael S. Hyatt. All rights reserved. Originally published at www.michaelhyatt.com."

ABOUT THE AUTHOR

In 2007, I self-published my first book. That was an educational eye-opener. For nearly a year, I researched the publishing process and was shocked at the things many online publishers will do to extract money from naïve, uninformed first-time authors. I almost went with one of those vanity publishers before I learned what bottom-feeders some of them are. I know that sounds harsh, but it is reality. Some of them will lie to your face.

A handful of publishing companies are sincerely trying to help authors self-publish with fair pricing and honest practices. They are the true self-publishing facilitators.

I wrote *Get Published without Getting Ripped Off* to help first-time authors avoid unscrupulous publishers. Writing is a passion—publishing is a business and you need to learn the difference or it will cost you dearly.

OTHER AVAILABLE BOOKS:

YOU HAVE ENOUGH FAITH
(Stop Asking for More)

To order Ted's books, go to:
http://www.jcpublishers.net
Also available from any online bookseller.

You can email ted@jcpublishers.net

Ted Bowman
4844 Osprey Way
Winter Haven, Florida 33881
863-875-6071

www.ingramcontent.com/pod-product-compliance
Lightning Source LLC
Chambersburg PA
CBHW070107070426
42448CB00038B/1837